BESIDE THE STILL WATERS

A CELEBRATION of BELOVED PSALMS

*The Green River in Bridger-Teton National Forest, Wyoming.
Photograph by Carr Clifton*

Beside the Still Waters

A Celebration of Beloved Psalms

Thy word is a lamp unto my feet,
and a light unto my path.
—Psalm 119:105

Melinda Rumbaugh, Editor

ideals

ISBN-13: 978-0-8249-5911-1

Published by Ideals Publications
A Guideposts Company
Nashville, Tennessee
www.idealsbooks.com

Printed and bound in the U.S.A.

Publisher, Peggy Schaefer
Editor, Melinda Rathjen Rumbaugh
Permissions Editor, Patsy Jay
Copy Editors, Debra Wright, Michelle Prater Burke

Designed by Marisa Jackson

Cover: Marsh-marigolds in Hasley Basin, in the White River National Forest, Colorado. Photograph by Carr Clifton

ADDITIONAL PHOTO CREDITS

Pages 5, 16–17, Photograph © Corbis; pages 6–7, farmland on the Palouse in Washington. Photograph by Dennis Frates; pages 10–11, maple branches in Great Smoky Mountains National Park, Tennessee. Photograph by Terry Donnelly/Donnelly-Austin Photography; pages 22–23, Photograph © age fotostock/SuperStock; pages 26–27, Tidal Lagoon, Aialik Bay, Kenai Fjords National Park, Alaska. Photograph by Carr Clifton; pages 30–31, Photograph © Comstock, Inc.; pages 36–37, Photograph © Corbis; pages 42–43, Panoramic view in Great Smoky Mountains National Park, Tennessee. Photograph © Emi Allen/SuperStock; pages 46–47, Sunrise on Queen's Bath, Kauai, Hawaii. Photograph by Dennis Frates; pages 50–51, Pink dogwood blossoms in Fountaindale, Pennsylvania. Photograph by William H. Johnson; pages 56–57, Photograph © Comstock, Inc.; pages 60–61, A cluster of lupine in the Finger Lakes Region of New York. Photograph by Carr Clifton; pages 64–65, Lake Powell, Glen Canyon National Recreation Area, Utah. Photograph by Carr Clifton; pages 70–71, Gooseberry Falls State Park, Minnesota. Photograph by Carr Clifton; pages 76–77, Photograph © istockphoto.com/DHuss; pages 86–87, Alpine wildflowers in Mount Rainier National Park, Washington. Photograph by Terry Donnelly/Donnelly-Austin Photography; pages 90–91, Fog clearing from Nuka Bay in Kenai Fjords National Park, Alaska. Photograph by Carr Clifton; pages 94–95, Photograph © Corbis; pages 98–99, Photograph © Corbis; pages 106–107, Photograph © istockphoto.com/brytta; pages 108–109, Moonrise and reflections on Crater Lake, Crater Lake National Park, Oregon. Photograph by Terry Donnelly/Donnelly-Austin Photography; pages 114–115, Dogwood in spring bloom in the Sierra Nevada foothills, California. Photograph by Jon Gnass; pages 120–121, Photograph © age fotostock/SuperStock; pages 126–127, Photograph © Corbis; pages 132–133, Tree in morning fog, Kauai, Hawaii. Photograph by Dennis Frates; pages 138–139, Photograph by Terry Donnelly/Donnelly-Austin Photography; pages 144–145, Winter dawn on the peaks of the Teton Range, Grand Teton National Park, Wyoming. Photograph by Terry Donnelly/Donnelly-Austin Photography; pages 152–153, Photograph by © age fotostock/SuperStock.

ACKNOWLEDGMENTS:

All Scripture quotations are taken from the *Holy Bible*, King James Version.

"How Great Thou Art." Copyright © 1953 by S. K. HINE. Renewed 1981. Administrator: Manna Music, Inc., 35255 Brooten Road, Pacific City, OR 97135. All rights reserved. Used by permission.

"Sometimes By Step." Words and music by DAVID "BEAKER" STRASSER. Copyright © 1992 by Universal Music - MGB Songs and Kid Brothers of St. Frank Publishing. This arrangement copyright © 2010 by Universal Music - MGB Songs and Kid Brothers of St. Frank Publishing. All rights administered by Universal Music - MGB Songs. International copyright secured. All rights reserved. Reprinted by permission of Hal Leonard Corporation.

BECKER, EDNA. "Reflections" reprinted in *Masterpieces of Religious Verse* by Harper & Brothers, 1948, and used here by permission of Christian Century. CARMICHAEL, AMY. "Hope", previously titled "God of Hope" from *Mountain Breezes*, Fort Washington, PA: CLC Publications, 1999. Used by permission of CLC Ministries. CROWELL, GRACE NOLL. "Eternal Assurance," "Vision," and "Facing the Stars" from *The Eternal Things*. Copyright © 1941, renewed 1970 by Reid Crowell. Reprinted by permission of HarperCollins Publishers. KELLER, HELEN. "Without This Faith" from *Midstream* by Helen Keller, copyright © 1929 by the author and the Crowell Publishing Company. Used by permission of Doubleday, a division of Random House, Inc. MERTON, THOMAS. "The Road Ahead" from *Thoughts in Solitude*, copyright © 1956, 1958 by the Abbey of Our Lady of Gethsemani. Renewal © 1986 by the Trustees of the Thomas Merton Legacy Trust. Published by Farrar, Straus and Giroux, LLC. "We Give Thee Thanks" reprinted in *A Thomas Merton Reader*, copyright © 1962 by the Abbey of Gethsemani Inc. Used by permission of the Merton Legacy Trust. OXENHAM, JOHN. "The Day—The Way" from *The Treasury of Religious Verse*, 1962, by permission of Miss Theo Oxenham and used here by permission of Desmond Dunkerley.

OUR SINCERE THANKS to the following authors or their heirs whom we were unable to contact: Augustus Wright Bamberger for "Out of the Vast," Ralph Spaulding Cushman for "I Will Not Hurry Through This Day!," Anna Blake Mezquida for "Hope," and Frederick George Scott for "Ad Majorem Dei Gloriam," all having been previously published in *Masterpieces of Religious Verse*, and to Ralph Spaulding Cushman for "Sheer Joy" in *The Treasury of Religious Verse*.

Every effort has been made to establish ownership and use of each selection in this book. If contacted, the publisher will be pleased to rectify any inadvertent errors or omissions in subsequent editions.

10 9 8 7 6 5 4 3 2 1

TABLE of CONTENTS

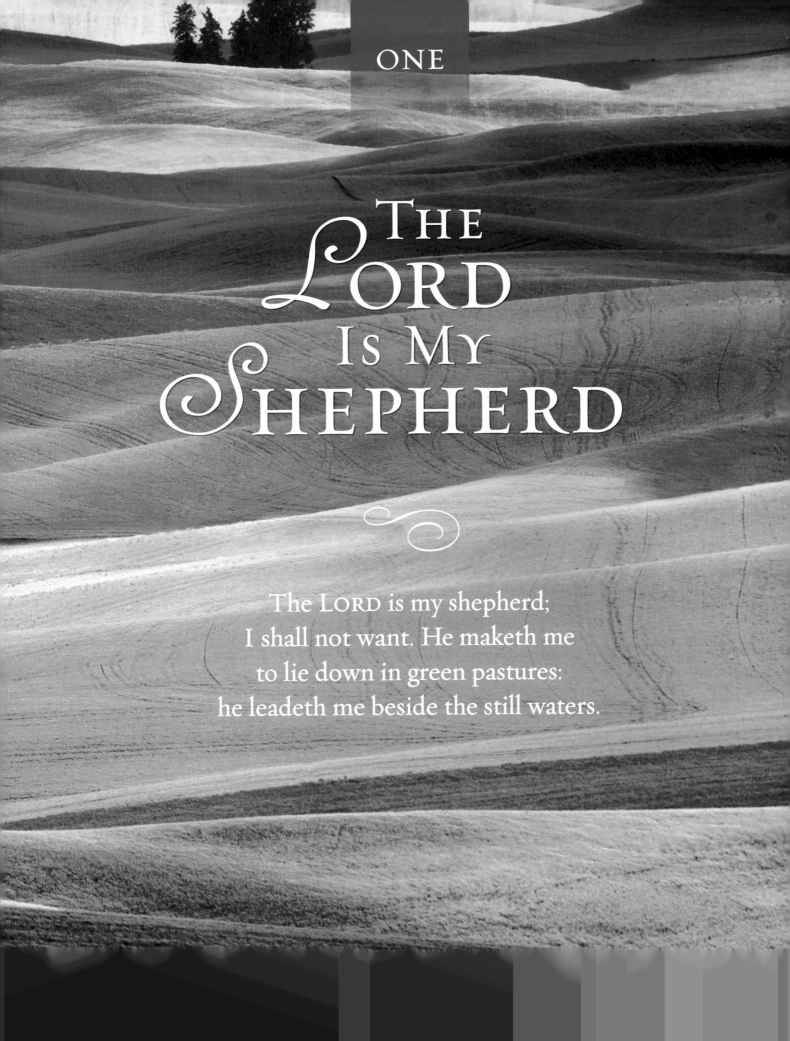

ONE

The Lord Is My Shepherd

The LORD is my shepherd;
I shall not want. He maketh me
to lie down in green pastures:
he leadeth me beside the still waters.

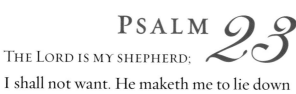

PSALM 23

THE LORD IS MY SHEPHERD;
I shall not want. He maketh me to lie down
in green pastures: he leadeth me beside the
still waters. He restoreth my soul: he leadeth me in the paths of righteousness for his
name's sake. Yea, though I walk through

---

*Surely goodness and
mercy shall follow me
all the days of my life. . . .*

---

the valley of the shadow of death, I will fear
no evil: for thou art with me; thy rod and
thy staff they comfort me. Thou preparest
a table before me in the presence of mine
enemies: thou anointest my head with oil;
my cup runneth over. Surely goodness and
mercy shall follow me all the days of my life:
and I will dwell in the house of the LORD
for ever.

*Mule's ears and geraniums on Antelope Flats
in Grand Teton National Park, Wyoming. Photograph by
Mary Liz Austin/Donnelly-Austin Photography*

THE LORD'S MY SHEPHERD

Psalm 23, Scottish Psalter, 1650   Arranged from William Havergal by Lowell Mason

PSALM *51*

HAVE MERCY UPON ME, O GOD, according to thy lovingkindness: according unto the multitude of thy tender mercies blot out my transgressions. Wash me throughly from mine iniquity, and cleanse me from my sin. For I acknowledge my transgressions: and my sin is ever before me. Against thee, thee only, have I sinned, and done this evil in thy sight: that thou mightest be justified when thou speakest, and be clear when thou judgest. Behold, I was shapen in iniquity; and in sin did my mother conceive me. Behold,

---

Create in me a clean heart, O God; and renew a right spirit within me.

---

thou desirest truth in the inward parts: and in the hidden part thou shalt make me to know wisdom. Purge me with hyssop, and I shall be clean: wash me, and I shall be whiter than snow. Make me to hear joy and gladness; that the bones which thou hast broken may rejoice. Hide thy face from my sins, and blot out all mine iniquities. Create in me a clean heart, O God; and renew a right spirit within me. Cast me not away from thy presence; and take not thy holy spirit from me. Restore unto me the joy of thy salvation; and uphold me with thy free spirit. Then will I teach transgressors thy ways; and sinners shall be converted unto thee. Deliver me from bloodguiltiness, O God, thou God of my salvation: and my tongue shall sing aloud of thy righteousness. O LORD, open thou my lips; and my mouth shall shew forth thy praise. For thou desirest not sacrifice; else would I give it: thou delightest not in burnt offering. The sacrifices of God are a broken spirit: a broken and a contrite heart, O God, thou wilt not despise. Do good in thy good pleasure unto Zion: build thou the walls of Jerusalem. (VERSES 1–18)

Big Thompson Creek and distant mountains in Rocky Mountain National Park, Colorado. Photograph by Mary Liz Austin/Donnelly-Austin Photography

PSALM *16*

PRESERVE ME, O GOD: for in thee do I put my trust. O my soul, thou hast said unto the LORD, Thou art my LORD: my goodness extendeth not to thee; But to the saints that are in the earth, and to the excellent, in whom is all my delight. Their sorrows shall be multiplied that hasten after another god: their drink offerings of blood will I not offer, nor take up their names into my lips.

The LORD is the portion of mine inheritance and of my

I will bless the LORD, who hath given me counsel . . .

cup: thou maintainest my lot. The lines are fallen unto me in pleasant places; yea, I have a goodly heritage.

I will bless the LORD, who hath given me counsel: my reins also instruct me in the night seasons.

I have set the LORD always before me: because he is at my right hand, I shall not be moved.

Therefore my heart is glad, and my glory rejoiceth: my flesh also shall rest in hope. For thou wilt not leave my soul in hell; neither wilt thou suffer thine Holy One to see corruption.

Thou wilt shew me the path of life: in thy presence is fulness of joy; at thy right hand there are pleasures for evermore.

Aspen and maples in Ottawa National Forest, Michigan.
Photograph by Carr Clifton

The King of Love

Henry W. Baker

The King of love my shepherd is,
Whose goodness faileth never;
I nothing lack if I am his,
And he is mine forever.

Where streams of living water flow
My ransomed soul he leadeth,
And where the verdant pastures grow
With food celestial feedeth.

Perverse and foolish oft I strayed,
But yet in love he sought me;
And on his shoulder gently laid
And home rejoicing brought me.

In death's dark vale I fear no ill
With thee, dear Lord, beside me,
Thy rod and staff my comfort still,
Thy cross before to guide me.

Thou spread'st a table in my sight,
Thy unction grace bestoweth,
And O what transport of delight
From thy pure chalice floweth.

And so through all the length of days
Thy goodness faileth never;
Good Shepherd, may I sing thy praise
Within thy house forever.

How excellent is thy
lovingkindness, O God!
therefore the children of
men put their trust under
the shadow of thy wings.

—PSALM 36:7

Prayer

John Wesley

O God, whose eternal providence
Has embarked our souls in our bodies,
Not to expect any port of anchorage
On the sea of this world,
To steer directly through it
To your glorious kingdom,
Preserve us from the dangers
That on all sides assault us,
And keep our affections
Still fitly disposed to receive
Your holy inspirations,
That being carried strongly forward
By your Holy Spirit
We may happily arrive at last
In the haven of our eternal salvation,
Through our Lord, Jesus Christ. Amen.

A Hymn

Paul Laurence Dunbar

Lead gently, Lord, and slow,
For oh, my steps are weak,
And ever as I go,
Some soothing sentence speak;

That I may turn my face
Through doubt's obscurity
Toward thine abiding-place,
E'en tho' I cannot see.

For lo, the way is dark;
Through mist and cloud I grope,
Save for that fitful spark,
The little flame of hope.

Lead gently, Lord, and slow,
For fear that I may fall;
I know not where to go
Unless I hear thy call.

My fainting soul doth yearn
For thy green hills afar;
So let thy mercy burn—
My greater, guiding star!

God Makes a Path

Roger Williams

God makes a path, provides a guide,
And feeds a wilderness;
His glorious name, while breath remains,
O that I may confess.

Lost many a time, I have had no guide,
No house but a hollow tree!
In stormy winter night no fire,
No food, no company.

In him I found a house, a bed,
A table, company;
No cup so bitter but's made sweet,
When God shall sweetening be.

I Will Not Hurry Through This Day!

Ralph Spaulding Cushman

I will not hurry through this day!
Lord, I will listen by the way
To humming bees and singing birds,
To speaking trees and friendly words;
And for the moments in between
Seek glimpses of thy great unseen.

I will not hurry through this day;
I will take the time to think and pray.
I will look up into the sky,
Where fleecy clouds and swallows fly;
And somewhere in the day, maybe
I will catch whispers, Lord, from thee!

PSALM 37

TRUST IN THE LORD, AND DO GOOD; so shalt thou dwell in the land, and verily thou shalt be fed.

Delight thyself also in the LORD; and he shall give thee the desires of thine heart. Commit thy way unto the LORD; trust also in him; and he shall bring it to pass. And he shall bring forth thy righteousness as the light, and thy judgment as the noonday.

Rest in the LORD, and wait patiently for him: fret not thyself because of him who prospereth in his way, because of the man

> But the meek shall inherit the earth;
> and shall delight themselves
> in the abundance of peace. . . .

who bringeth wicked devices to pass. Cease from anger, and forsake wrath: fret not thyself in any wise to do evil. For evildoers shall be cut off: but those that wait upon the LORD, they shall inherit the earth. For yet a little while, and the wicked shall not be: yea, thou shalt diligently consider his place, and it shall not be.

But the meek shall inherit the earth; and shall delight themselves in the abundance of peace. . . .

The LORD knoweth the days of the upright: and their inheritance shall be for ever. They shall not be ashamed in the evil time: and in the days of famine they shall be satisfied. . . .

The steps of a good man are ordered by the LORD: and he delighteth in his way. Though he fall, he shall not be utterly cast down: for the LORD upholdeth him with his hand. I have been young, and now am old; yet have I not seen the righteous forsaken, nor his seed begging bread. He is ever merciful, and lendeth; and his seed is blessed. Depart from evil, and do good; and dwell for evermore. . . . (VERSES 3–11, 18–19, 23–27)

Sandstone rocks at Red Rock Canyon State Park, California. Photograph by Dennis Frates

PSALM 25

UNTO THEE, O LORD, DO I LIFT UP MY SOUL. O my God, I trust in thee: let me not be ashamed, let not mine enemies triumph over me. Yea, let none that wait on thee be ashamed: let them be ashamed which transgress without cause. Shew me thy ways, O LORD; teach me thy paths.

Lead me in thy truth, and teach me: for thou art the God of my salvation; on thee do I wait all the day. Remember, O LORD, thy tender mercies and thy lovingkindnesses; for they have been ever

Lead me in thy truth, and teach me . . .

of old. Remember not the sins of my youth, nor my transgressions: according to thy mercy remember thou me for thy goodness' sake, O LORD. Good and upright is the LORD: therefore will he teach sinners in the way. The meek will he guide in judgment: and the meek will he teach his way. All the paths of the LORD are mercy and truth unto such as keep his covenant and his testimonies. For thy name's sake, O LORD, pardon mine iniquity; for it is great. What man is he that feareth the LORD? him shall he teach in the way that he shall choose. His soul shall dwell at ease; and his seed shall inherit the earth. The secret of the LORD is with them that fear him; and he will shew them his covenant.

Mine eyes are ever toward the LORD; for he shall pluck my feet out of the net. Turn thee unto me, and have mercy upon me; for I am desolate and afflicted. The troubles of my heart are enlarged: O bring thou me out of my distresses. Look upon mine affliction and my pain; and forgive all my sins. . . .

O keep my soul, and deliver me: let me not be ashamed; for I put my trust in thee. Let integrity and uprightness preserve me; for I wait on thee. (VERSES 1–18, 20–21)

Iris in Allegany State Park, New York. Photograph by Carr Clifton

Prayer

Saint Thomas Aquinas

O Creator past all telling,
You have appointed
From the treasures of your wisdom
The hierarchies of angels,
Disposing them in wondrous order
Above the bright heavens,

And have so beautifully set out
All parts of the universe.
You we call the true fount of wisdom
And the noble origin of all things.

Be pleased to shed
On the darkness of mind in which I was born
The twofold beam of your light
And warmth to dispel my ignorance and sin.
You make eloquent the tongues of children.

Then instruct my speech
And touch my lips with graciousness.
Make me keen to understand,
Quick to learn, able to remember;

Make me delicate to interpret
    and ready to speak,
Guide my going in and going forward,
Lead home my going forth.
You are true God and true man
And live forever and ever.

The Road Ahead

Thomas Merton

My Lord, God,
I have no idea where I am going.
I do not see the road ahead of me.
I cannot know for certain
    where it will end.
Nor do I really know myself,
And the fact that I think
That I am following your will
Does not mean that I am
    actually doing so.
But I believe that the desire
    to please you
Does in fact please you,
And I hope I have that desire
    in all that I am doing.

I hope that I will never do anything
Apart from that desire.
And I know that if I do this,
You will lead me by the right road,
Though I may know nothing about it.
Therefore will I trust you always
Though I may seem to be lost
In the shadow of death.
I will not fear, for you are ever with me,
And you will never leave me
    to face my perils alone.

The Day—the Way

John Oxenham

Not for one single day
Can I discern my way,
But this I surely know—
Who gives the day
Will show the way,
So I securely go.

Trust in the LORD, and do good;
so shalt thou dwell in the land, and
verily thou shalt be fed. Delight thyself
also in the LORD; and he shall give
thee the desires of thine heart.

—PSALM 37:3–4

A Prayer

Saint Augustine

Blessed are all your saints,
O God and King, who have traveled
over the tempestuous sea of this life
and have made the harbor of peace and felicity.

Watch over us
who are still on our dangerous voyage;
and remember those who lie exposed to
the rough storms of trouble and temptations.

Frail is our vessel, and the ocean is wide;
but as in your memory you have set our course,
so steer the vessel of our life towards
the everlasting shore of peace,
and bring us at length
to the quiet haven of our heart's desire,
where you, O God,
are blessed and live and reign forever.

How Gentle God's Commands

Philip Doddridge

How gentle God's commands,
How kind his precepts are!
Come, cast your burdens on the Lord,
And trust his constant care.

Beneath his watchful eye,
His saints securely dwell;
That hand which bears all nature up
Shall guide his children well.

Why should this anxious load
Press down your weary mind?
Haste to your heavenly Father's throne,
And sweet refreshment find.

His goodness stands approved,
Unchanged from day to day;
I'll drop my burden at his feet
And bear a song away.

PSALM *139*

O LORD, THOU HAST SEARCHED ME, and known me. Thou knowest my downsitting and mine uprising, thou understandest my thought afar off. Thou compassest my path and my lying down, and art acquainted with all my ways. For there is not a word in my tongue, but, lo, O LORD, thou knowest it altogether.

Thou hast beset me behind and before, and laid thine hand upon me. Such knowledge is too wonderful for me; it is high, I cannot attain unto it.

Thou hast searched me, and known me.

Whither shall I go from thy spirit? or whither shall I flee from thy presence? If I ascend up into heaven, thou art there: if I make my bed in hell, behold, thou art there. If I take the wings of the morning, and dwell in the uttermost parts of the sea; Even there shall thy hand lead me, and thy right hand shall hold me.

If I say, Surely the darkness shall cover me; even the night shall be light about me. Yea, the darkness hideth not from thee; but the night shineth as the day: the darkness and the light are both alike to thee.

For thou hast possessed my reins: thou hast covered me in my mother's womb. I will praise thee; for I am fearfully and wonderfully made: marvellous are thy works; and that my soul knoweth right well. My substance was not hid from thee, when I was made in secret, and curiously wrought in the lowest parts of the earth. . . .

How precious also are thy thoughts unto me, O God! how great is the sum of them! If I should count them, they are more in number than the sand: when I awake, I am still with thee.

(VERSES 1–15, 17–18)

Bald cypress swamp in Merchants Millpond State Park, North Carolina. Photograph by Carr Clifton

TWO

As the Hart Panteth for the Water

As the hart panteth
after the water brooks, so
panteth my soul after thee, O God.

PSALM 42

AS THE HART PANTETH after the water brooks, so panteth my soul after thee, O God. My soul thirsteth for God, for the living God: when shall I come and appear before God? My tears have been my meat day and night, while they continually say unto me, Where is thy God? When I remember these things, I pour out my soul in me: for I had gone with the multitude, I went with them to the house of God, with the voice of joy and praise, with a multitude that kept holyday.

Hope thou in God; for I shall yet praise him . . .

Why art thou cast down, O my soul? and why art thou disquieted in me? hope thou in God: for I shall yet praise him for the help of his countenance. O my God, my soul is cast down within me: therefore will I remember thee from the land of Jordan, and of the Hermonites, from the hill Mizar. Deep calleth unto deep at the noise of thy waterspouts: all thy waves and thy billows are gone over me.

Yet the Lord will command his lovingkindness in the daytime, and in the night his song shall be with me, and my prayer unto the God of my life. I will say unto God my rock, Why hast thou forgotten me? why go I mourning because of the oppression of the enemy? As with a sword in my bones, mine enemies reproach me; while they say daily unto me, Where is thy God? Why art thou cast down, O my soul? and why art thou disquieted within me? hope thou in God: for I shall yet praise him, who is the health of my countenance, and my God.

North Fork Silver Creek in Silver Falls State Park, Oregon. Photograph by Dennis Frates

Vestigia

Bliss Carman

I took a day to search for God
And found him not. But as I trod
By rocky ledge, through woods untamed,
Just where one scarlet lily flamed,
I saw his footprint in the sod.

Then suddenly, all unaware,
Far off in the deep shadows—where
A solitary hermit thrush
Sang through the holy twilight hush—
I heard his voice upon the air.

And even as I marveled how
God gives us heaven here and now,
In a stir of wind that hardly shook
The poplar leaves beside the brook—
His hand was light upon my brow.

At last with evening as I turned
Homeward—and thought what I
    had learned
And all that there was still to probe—
I caught the glory of his robe
Where the last fires of sunset burned.

Back to the world with quickening start
I looked and longed for any part
In making saving beauty be . . .
And from that kindling ecstasy
I knew God dwelt within my heart.

As for me, I will call upon God;
   and the LORD shall save me.
Evening, and morning, and
   at noon, will I pray, and cry
aloud: and he shall hear my voice.

—PSALM 55:16–17

Lost and Found

George Macdonald

I missed him when the sun began to bend;
I found him not when I had lost his rim;
With many tears I went in search of him,
Climbing high mountains which
    did still ascend
And gave me echoes when I called my friend;
Through cities vast and charnel-houses grim
And high cathedrals where the light was dim,
Through books and arts and works
    without an end,
But found him not—the friend
    whom I had lost.
And yet I found him—as I found the lark,
A sound in fields I heard but could not mark;
I found him nearest when I missed him most;
I found him in my heart, a life in frost,
A light I knew not till my soul was dark.

Walking with God

William Cowper

Oh! for a closer walk with God,
A calm and heavenly frame;
A light to shine upon the road
That leads me to the Lamb!

Where is the blessedness I knew
When first I saw the Lord?
Where is the soul-refreshing view
Of Jesus and his word?

What peaceful hours I once enjoyed!
How sweet their memory still!
But they have left an aching void
The world can never fill.

Return, O holy Dove, return,
Sweet messenger of rest!
I hate the sins that made thee mourn
And drove thee from my breast.

The dearest idol I have known,
Whate'er that idol be,
Help me to tear it from thy throne
And worship only thee.

So shall my walk be close with God,
Calm and serene my frame;
So purer light shall mark the road
That leads me to the Lamb.

Round Our Restlessness

Elizabeth Barrett Browning

Oh, the little birds sang east, and the little birds sang west,
And I smiled to think God's greatness flowed around
　　our incompleteness—
Round our restlessness, his rest.

Easter Wings

George Herbert

Lord, who createdst man in wealth and store,
　　Though foolishly he lost the same,
　　　　Decaying more and more,
　　　　　　Till he became
　　　　　　　　Most poor:
　　　　　　　　　With thee
　　　　　　　　O let me rise
　　　　　　As larks, harmoniously,
　　　　And sing this day thy victories:
Then shall the fall further the flight in me.

My tender age in sorrow did begin:
　　And still with sicknesses and shame
　　　　Thou didst so punish sin,
　　　　　　That I became
　　　　　　　　Most thin.
　　　　　　　　　With thee
　　　　　　　　Let me combine
　　　　　　And feel this day thy victory:
　　　　For if I imp my wing on thine,
Affliction shall advance the flight in me.

PSALM 17

HEAR THE RIGHT, O LORD, attend unto my cry, give ear unto my prayer, that goeth not out of feigned lips. Let my sentence come forth from thy presence; let thine eyes behold the things that are equal. Thou hast proved mine heart; thou hast visited me in the night; thou hast tried me, and shalt find nothing; I am purposed that my mouth shall not transgress. Concerning the works of men, by the word of thy lips I have kept me from

Keep me as the apple of the eye . . .

the paths of the destroyer. Hold up my goings in thy paths, that my footsteps slip not.

I have called upon thee, for thou wilt hear me, O God: incline thine ear unto me, and hear my speech. Shew thy marvellous lovingkindness, O thou that savest by thy right hand them which put their trust in thee from those that rise up against them.

Keep me as the apple of the eye, hide me under the shadow of thy wings, From the wicked that oppress me, from my deadly enemies, who compass me about. They are inclosed in their own fat: with their mouth they speak proudly. They have now compassed us in our steps: they have set their eyes bowing down to the earth; Like as a lion that is greedy of his prey, and as it were a young lion lurking in secret places.

Arise, O LORD, disappoint him, cast him down: deliver my soul from the wicked, which is thy sword: From men which are thy hand, O LORD, from men of the world, which have their portion in this life, and whose belly thou fillest with thy hid treasure: they are full of children, and leave the rest of their substance to their babes.

As for me, I will behold thy face in righteousness: I shall be satisfied, when I awake, with thy likeness.

Mount Rainier towering over alpine flowers on Mazama Ridge in Mount Rainier National Park, Washington. Photograph by Terry Donnelly/Donnelly-Austin Photography

PSALM 86

BOW DOWN THINE EAR, O LORD, hear me: for I am poor and needy. Preserve my soul; for I am holy: O thou my God, save thy servant that trusteth in thee.

Be merciful unto me, O LORD: for I cry unto thee daily. Rejoice the soul of thy servant: for unto thee, O LORD, do I lift up my soul. For thou, LORD, art good, and ready to forgive; and plenteous in mercy unto all them that call upon thee. Give ear, O LORD, unto my prayer; and attend to the voice of my supplications. In the day of my trouble I will call upon thee: for thou wilt answer me.

Teach me thy way, O LORD. . . .

Among the gods there is none like unto thee, O LORD; neither are there any works like unto thy works. All nations whom thou hast made shall come and worship before thee, O LORD; and shall glorify thy name. For thou art great, and doest wondrous things: thou art God alone. Teach me thy way, O LORD; I will walk in thy truth: unite my heart to fear thy name.

I will praise thee, O LORD my God, with all my heart: and I will glorify thy name for evermore. For great is thy mercy toward me: and thou hast delivered my soul from the lowest hell. O God, the proud are risen against me, and the assemblies of violent men have sought after my soul; and have not set thee before them. But thou, O LORD, art a God full of compassion, and gracious, longsuffering, and plenteous in mercy and truth.

O turn unto me, and have mercy upon me; give thy strength unto thy servant, and save the son of thine handmaid. Shew me a token for good; that they which hate me may see it, and be ashamed: because thou, LORD, hast holpen me, and comforted me.

Sandstone cliffs in the Garden of the Gods Recreation Area of the Shawnee National Forest, Illinois. Photograph by Terry Donnelly/Donnelly-Austin Photography

SOMETIMES BY STEP

David Strasser   David Strasser

Oh   God,   you are   my   God,   and

I   will   ev - er praise   You;   Oh

God,   You are   my   God,   and

I   will   ev - er praise   You.   I will

seek You in the morn - ing, and I will

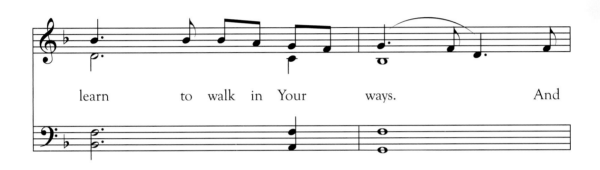

learn to walk in Your ways. And

step by step You lead me, and I will

fol - low You all of my days.

PSALM 63

O GOD, THOU ART MY GOD; early will I seek thee: my soul thirsteth for thee, my flesh longeth for thee in a dry and thirsty land, where no water is; To see thy power and thy glory, so as I have seen thee in the sanctuary. Because thy lovingkindness is better than life, my lips shall praise thee. Thus will I bless thee while I live: I will lift up

---

Because thy lovingkindness is better than life, my lips shall praise thee.

---

my hands in thy name. My soul shall be satisfied as with marrow and fatness; and my mouth shall praise thee with joyful lips: When I remember thee upon my bed, and meditate on thee in the night watches. Because thou hast been my help, therefore in the shadow of thy wings will I rejoice. My soul followeth hard after thee: thy right hand upholdeth me. But those that seek my soul, to destroy it, shall go into the lower parts of the earth. They shall fall by the sword: they shall be a portion for foxes. But the king shall rejoice in God; every one that sweareth by him shall glory: but the mouth of them that speak lies shall be stopped.

A field of wildflowers in Olsztynek, Poland.
Photograph by Travel Library Limited/SuperStock

PSALM *84*

HOW AMIABLE ARE THY TABERNACLES, O LORD of hosts! My soul longeth, yea, even fainteth for the courts of the LORD: my heart and my flesh crieth out for the living God. Yea, the sparrow hath found an house, and the swallow a nest for herself, where she may lay her young, even thine altars, O LORD of hosts, my King, and my God. Blessed are they that dwell in thy house: they will be still praising thee. Selah.

Blessed are they that dwell in thy house: they will be still praising thee.

Blessed is the man whose strength is in thee; in whose heart are the ways of them. Who passing through the valley of Baca make it a well; the rain also filleth the pools. They go from strength to strength, every one of them in Zion appeareth before God. O LORD God of hosts, hear my prayer: give ear, O God of Jacob. Selah.

Behold, O God our shield, and look upon the face of thine anointed. For a day in thy courts is better than a thousand. I had rather be a doorkeeper in the house of my God, than to dwell in the tents of wickedness. For the LORD God is a sun and shield: the LORD will give grace and glory: no good thing will he withhold from them that walk uprightly. O LORD of hosts, blessed is the man that trusteth in thee.

Sunrise over Padre Island National Seashore, Texas.
Photograph by Terry Donnelly/Donnelly-Austin Photography

Intuition
FROM "IN MEMORIAM"

Alfred, Lord Tennyson

That which we dare invoke to bless;
Our dearest faith; our ghastliest doubt;
He, They, One, All; within, without;
The Power in darkness whom we guess;

I found him not in world or sun,
Or eagle's wings, or insect's eye;
Nor thro' the questions men may try,
The petty cobwebs we have spun.

If e'er when faith had fall'n asleep,
I heard a voice "Believe no more"
And heard an ever-breaking shore
That tumbled in the Godless deep;

A warmth within the breast would melt
The freezing reason's colder part,
And like a man in wrath the heart
Stood up and answer'd "I have felt."

No, like a child in doubt and fear:
But that blind clamor made me wise;
Then was I as a child that cries,
But, crying, knows his father near;

And what I am beheld again
What is, and no man understands;
And out of darkness came the hands
That reach thro' nature, moulding men.

Hear my prayer, O God; give ear to the words of my mouth.
—PSALM 54:2

An Empty Vessel
Martin Luther

Behold, Lord, an empty vessel
That needs to be filled.
My Lord, fill it. I am weak in faith;
Strengthen thou me. I am cold in love;
Warm me and make me fervent
That my love may go out to my neighbor.

I do not have a strong and firm faith;
At times I doubt and am unable
To trust thee altogether.
O Lord, help me.
Strengthen my faith and trust in thee.
In thee I have sealed the treasures of all I have.

I am poor; thou art rich
And didst come to be merciful to the poor.
I am a sinner; thou art merciful and upright.
With me there is an abundance of sin;
In thee is the fullness of righteousness.

Therefore, I will remain with thee
Of whom I can receive
But to whom I may not give.
Amen.

Love Divine, All Loves Excelling

Charles Wesley

Love divine, all loves excelling,
Joy of heaven, to earth come down;
Fix in us thy humble dwelling;
All thy faithful mercies crown.
Jesus, thou art all compassion,
Pure unbounded love thou art;
Visit us in thy salvation;
Enter every trembling heart.

Breathe, O breathe thy loving Spirit
Into every troubled breast;
Let us all in thee inherit;
Let us find that second rest.
Take away our power of sinning;
Alpha and Omega be;
End of faith as its beginning,
Set our hearts at liberty.

Finish, then, thy new creation;
Pure and spotless let us be.
Let us see thy great salvation
Perfectly restored in thee,
Changed from glory into glory
Till in heaven we take our place,
Till we cast our crowns before thee,
Lost in wonder, love, and praise!

Whoso Draws Nigh to God

Author Unknown

Whoso draws nigh to God
    one step
Through doubtings dim,
God will advance a mile
In blazing light to him.

I Sought the Lord

Author Unknown

I sought the Lord, and afterward I knew
He moved my soul to seek him, seeking me.
It was not I that found, O Saviour true;
No, I was found of thee.

Thou didst reach forth thy hand
    and mine enfold;
I walked and sank not on
    the storm-vexed sea.
'Twas not so much that I
    on thee took hold,
As thou, dear Lord, on me.

I find, I walk, I love, but oh, the whole
Of love is but my answer, Lord, to thee;
For thou were long before-hand
    with my soul,
Always thou lovedst me.

PSALM 143

HEAR MY PRAYER, O LORD, give ear to my supplications: in thy faithfulness answer me, and in thy righteousness. And enter not into judgment with thy servant: for in thy sight shall no man living be justified. For the enemy hath persecuted my soul; he hath smitten my life down to the ground; he hath made me to dwell in darkness, as those that have been long dead. Therefore is my spirit overwhelmed within me; my heart within me is desolate.

Deliver me, O LORD, from mine enemies: I flee unto thee to hide me.

I remember the days of old; I meditate on all thy works; I muse on the work of thy hands. I stretch forth my hands unto thee: my soul thirsteth after thee, as a thirsty land. Selah.

Hear me speedily, O LORD: my spirit faileth: hide not thy face from me, lest I be like unto them that go down into the pit. Cause me to hear thy lovingkindness in the morning; for in thee do I trust: cause me to know the way wherein I should walk; for I lift up my soul unto thee.

Deliver me, O LORD, from mine enemies: I flee unto thee to hide me. Teach me to do thy will; for thou art my God: thy spirit is good; lead me into the land of uprightness. Quicken me, O LORD, for thy name's sake: for thy righteousness' sake bring my soul out of trouble. And of thy mercy cut off mine enemies, and destroy all them that afflict my soul: for I am thy servant.

South Falls in Silver Falls State Park, Oregon.
Photograph by Terry Donnelly/Donnelly-Austin Photography

THREE

JOY COMETH
IN THE
MORNING

Thou hast turned for me
my mourning into dancing.

PSALM *30*

I WILL EXTOL THEE, O LORD; for thou hast lifted me up, and hast not made my foes to rejoice over me.

O LORD my God, I cried unto thee, and thou hast healed me. O LORD, thou hast brought up my soul from the grave: thou hast kept me alive, that I should not go down to the pit. Sing unto the LORD, O ye saints of his,

---

. . . weeping may endure for a night, but joy cometh in the morning.

---

and give thanks at the remembrance of his holiness. For his anger endureth but a moment; in his favour is life: weeping may endure for a night, but joy cometh in the morning. And in my prosperity I said, I shall never be moved. LORD, by thy favour thou hast made my mountain to stand strong: thou didst hide thy face, and I was troubled. I cried to thee, O LORD; and unto the LORD I made supplication. What profit is there in my blood, when I go down to the pit? Shall the dust praise thee? shall it declare thy truth?

Hear, O LORD, and have mercy upon me: LORD, be thou my helper. Thou hast turned for me my mourning into dancing: thou hast put off my sackcloth, and girded me with gladness; To the end that my glory may sing praise to thee, and not be silent. O LORD my God, I will give thanks unto thee for ever.

Arrowleaf balsam root and vetch under Oregon oaks in
Columbia Gorge National Scenic Area, Oregon.
Photograph by Terry Donnelly/Donnelly-Austin Photography

AMAZING GRACE

John Newton

Early American melody

1. A - maz - ing grace! How sweet the sound That saved a wretch like
2. 'Twas grace that taught my heart to fear, And grace my fears re -
3. The Lord has prom - ised good to me; His word my hope read -
4. Thro' man - y dan - gers, toils and snares, I have al - ready
5. When we've been there ten thou - sand years, Bright shin - ing as the

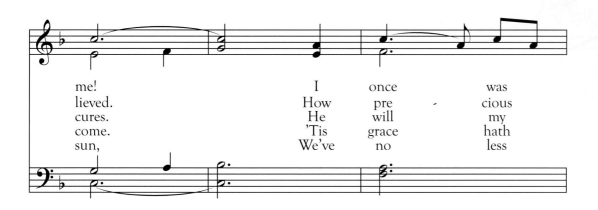

me!
lieved.
cures.
come.
sun,

I once was
How pre - cious
He will my
'Tis grace hath
We've no less

lost but now am found; Was
did that grace ap - pear The
shield and por - tion be As
bro't me safe thus far, And
days to sing God's praise Than

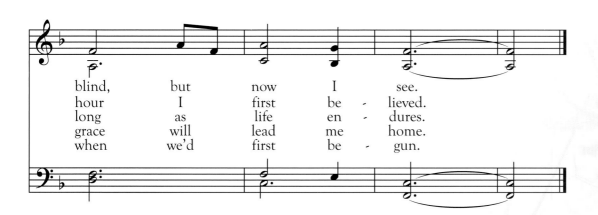

blind, but now I see.
hour I first be - lieved.
long as life en - dures.
grace will lead me home.
when we'd first be - gun.

PSALM *130*

OUT OF THE DEPTHS have I cried unto thee, O LORD. LORD, hear my voice: let thine ears be attentive to the voice of my supplications. If thou, LORD, shouldest mark iniquities, O LORD, who shall stand? But there is forgiveness with thee, that thou mayest be feared.

My soul waiteth for the LORD more than they that watch for the morning. . . .

I wait for the LORD, my soul doth wait, and in his word do I hope. My soul waiteth for the LORD more than they that watch for the morning: I say, more than they that watch for the morning. Let Israel hope in the LORD: for with the LORD there is mercy, and with him is plenteous redemption. And he shall redeem Israel from all his iniquities.

Snow-covered pines on Trapps Ridge, Shawangunk Mountains, Mohonk Preserve, New York. Photograph by Carr Clifton

PSALM *121*

I WILL LIFT UP MINE EYES unto the hills, from whence cometh my help. My help cometh from the LORD, which made heaven and earth. He will not suffer thy foot to be moved: he that keepeth thee will not slumber. Behold, he that keepeth Israel shall neither slumber nor sleep.

My help cometh from the LORD, which made heaven and earth.

The LORD is thy keeper: the LORD is thy shade upon thy right hand. The sun shall not smite thee by day, nor the moon by night. The LORD shall preserve thee from all evil: he shall preserve thy soul. The LORD shall preserve thy going out and thy coming in from this time forth, and even for evermore.

The San Juan Mountains and Archuleta Lake, Weminuche Wilderness, San Juan National Forest, Colorado. Photograph by Carr Clifton

Hope

Anna Blake Mezquida

I shall wear laughter on my lips
Though in my heart is pain—
God's sun is always brightest after rain.

I shall go singing down my little way
Though in my breast the dull ache grows—
The song birds come again after the snows.

I shall walk eager still for what life holds
Although it seems the hard road will not end—
One never knows the beauty round the bend!

Why art thou cast down,
O my soul? and why art
thou disquieted within me?
hope in God: for I shall yet
praise him, who is the
health of my countenance,
and my God.

—PSALM 43:5

Joy and Peace in Believing

William Cowper

Sometimes a light surprises
The Christian while he sings;
It is the Lord who rises
With healing on his wings;
When comforts are declining,
He grants the soul again
A season of clear shining,
To cheer it after rain.

In holy contemplation,
We sweetly then pursue
The theme of God's salvation
And find it ever new;

Set free from present sorrow
We cheerfully can say,
E'en let the unknown tomorrow
Bring with it what it may!

It can bring with it nothing,
But he will bear us through;
Who gives the lilies clothing,
Will clothe his people too;
Beneath the spreading heavens
No creature but is fed;
And he who feeds the ravens
Will give his children bread.

Though vine nor fig tree neither
Their wonted fruit shall bear,
Though all the field
    should wither,
Nor flocks nor herds be there:
Yet God the same abiding,
His praise shall tune my voice;
For while in him confiding,
I cannot but rejoice.

Without This Faith

Helen Keller

Without this faith
There would be little meaning in my life.
I should be
"A mere pillar of darkness in the dark."

Observers in the full enjoyment
Of their bodily senses pity me,
But it is because
They do not see
The golden chamber in my life
Where I dwell delighted;
For, dark as my path may seem to them,
I carry a magic light in my heart.

Faith, the spiritual strong searchlight,
Illumines the way,
And although sinister doubts
Lurk in the shadow,
I walk unafraid
Toward the Enchanted Wood
Where the foliage is always green,
Where joy abides,
Where nightingales nest and sing,
And where life and death are one
In the presence of the Lord.

Hope

Amy Carmichael

Great God of hope, how green thy trees,
How calm each several star.
Renew us; make us fresh as these,
Calm as those are.

For what can dim his hope who sees,
Though faintly and afar,
The power that kindles green in trees
And light in star?

Facing the Stars

Grace Noll Crowell

No matter how dark the night,
    how deep the shadows,
Still up beyond the cloud's obscuring bars,
Steadfast and silent, safe within God's keeping,
Move the radiant, self-illumined stars.

So I shall face skyward though the blackness
Sheds not one ray of light upon the air.
I know that back of the overhanging darkness
The white unfailing stars are ever there,

Moving by God's remote control and taking
Their clearly outlined courses, swift and free.
It comforts me to know that same great power
Controls my heart, my life, my destiny.

PSALM 107

O GIVE THANKS UNTO THE LORD, for he is good: for his mercy endureth for ever. Let the redeemed of the LORD say so, whom he hath redeemed from the hand of the enemy; And gathered them out of the lands, from the east, and from the west, from the north, and from the south. They wandered in the wilderness in a solitary way; they found no city to dwell in. Hungry and thirsty, their soul fainted in them. Then they cried unto the LORD in their trouble, and he delivered them out of their distresses. And he led

For he satisfieth the longing soul . . .

them forth by the right way, that they might go to a city of habitation. O that men would praise the LORD for his goodness, and for his wonderful works to the children of men! For he satisfieth the longing soul, and filleth the hungry soul with goodness. . . .

He turneth rivers into a wilderness, and the watersprings into dry ground; A fruitful land into barrenness, for the wickedness of them that dwell therein. He turneth the wilderness into a standing water, and dry ground into watersprings. And there he maketh the hungry to dwell, that they may prepare a city for habitation; And sow the fields, and plant vineyards, which may yield fruits of increase. He blesseth them also, so that they are multiplied greatly; and suffereth not their cattle to decrease. Again, they are minished and brought low through oppression, affliction, and sorrow. He poureth contempt upon princes, and causeth them to wander in the wilderness, where there is no way. Yet setteth he the poor on high from affliction, and maketh him families like a flock. The righteous shall see it, and rejoice: and all iniquity shall stop her mouth. Whoso is wise, and will observe these things, even they shall understand the lovingkindness of the LORD. (VERSES 1–9, 33–43)

Trail through trillium in Selkirk Shores State Park, New York. Photograph by Carr Clifton

King of Glory

George Herbert

King of Glory, King of Peace,
I will love thee;
And that love may never cease,
I will move thee.

Thou hast granted my request,
Thou hast heard me;
Thou didst note my
    working breast,
Thou hast spared me.

Wherefore with my
    utmost art
I will sing thee,

And the cream of all my heart
I will bring thee.

Though my sins against me cried,
Thou didst clear me;
And alone, when they replied,
Thou didst hear me.

Seven whole days, not one
    in seven,
I will praise thee.
In my heart, though not
    in heaven,
I can raise thee.

Thou grewst soft and moist
    with tears,
Thou relentedst;
And when Justice called
    for fears,
Thou dissentedst.

Small it is, in this poor sort
To enrol thee;
Even eternity is too short
To extol thee.

Ad Majorem Dei Gloriam

Frederick George Scott

Thy glory alone, O God, be the end
    of all that I say;
Let it shine in every deed, let it kindle
    the prayers that I pray;
Let it burn in my innermost soul, till the
    shadow of self pass away,
And the light of thy glory, O God, be unveiled
    in the dawning of day.

Reflections

Edna Becker

Stars lie broken on a lake
Whenever passing breezes make
The wavelets leap;
But when the lake is still, the sky
Gives moon and stars that they may lie
On that calm deep.

If, like the lake that has the boon
Of cradling the little moon
Above the hill,
I want the Infinite to be
Reflected undisturbed in me,
I must be still.

For with thee is the fountain of life:
in thy light shall we see light.

—PSALM 36:9

A Prayer

Phillips Brooks

O Lord,
By all your dealings with us,
Whether of joy or pain,
Of light or darkness,
Let us be brought to you.
Let us value no treatment of your grace
Simply because it makes us happy
Or because it makes us sad,
Because it gives us or denies us
    what we want;
But may all that you send us bring
    us to you,
That knowing your perfectness,
We may be sure in every disappointment
You are still loving us,
In every darkness
You are still enlightening us,
And in every enforced idleness
You are giving us life,
As in his death
You gave life to your Son,
Our Saviour, Jesus Christ.
Amen.

Sunrise

Margaret E. Sangster

Though the midnight
    found us weary,
The morning brings us cheer;
Thank God for every sunrise
In the circuit of the year.

Vision

Grace Noll Crowell

If we could see beyond a present sorrow,
Beyond a present grief, as God can see,
We would be braver, knowing some tomorrow
Will still hold happiness for you and me.

If our blurred eyes could glimpse
    beyond their weeping,
The sunlit hills that someday we shall climb,
We would be stronger, and we would be keeping
A tryst with Hope through every darkened time.

If we could see beyond a fresh disaster,
The road smoothed out again before our eyes,
We would be calmer, and we would learn faster
The lessons life unfolds to make us wise.

We are so blinded by a moment's grieving,
So hurt by any sorrow, any pain,
That we forget the joys, beyond believing,
The peace that someday will be ours again.

PSALM *116*

I LOVE THE LORD, because he hath heard my voice and my supplications. Because he hath inclined his ear unto me, therefore will I call upon him as long as I live.

The sorrows of death compassed me, and the pains of hell gat hold upon me: I found trouble and sorrow. Then called I upon the name of the LORD; O LORD, I beseech thee, deliver my soul. Gracious is the LORD, and righteous; yea, our God is merciful.

The LORD preserveth the simple: I was brought low, and he helped me. Return unto thy rest, O my soul; for the LORD hath

---

. . . he hath inclined his ear unto me . . .

---

dealt bountifully with thee. For thou hast delivered my soul from death, mine eyes from tears, and my feet from falling.

I will walk before the LORD in the land of the living. I believed, therefore have I spoken: I was greatly afflicted: I said in my haste, All men are liars.

What shall I render unto the LORD for all his benefits toward me? I will take the cup of salvation, and call upon the name of the LORD. I will pay my vows unto the LORD now in the presence of all his people. Precious in the sight of the LORD is the death of his saints. O LORD, truly I am thy servant; I am thy servant, and the son of thine handmaid: thou hast loosed my bonds. I will offer to thee the sacrifice of thanksgiving, and will call upon the name of the LORD. I will pay my vows unto the LORD now in the presence of all his people.

In the courts of the LORD'S house, in the midst of thee, O Jerusalem. Praise ye the LORD.

A winter storm clearing over North Cascade peaks and North Fork
Nooksack River Valley, Mt. Baker-Snoqualmie National Forest, Washington.
Photograph by Terry Donnelly/Donnelly-Austin Photography

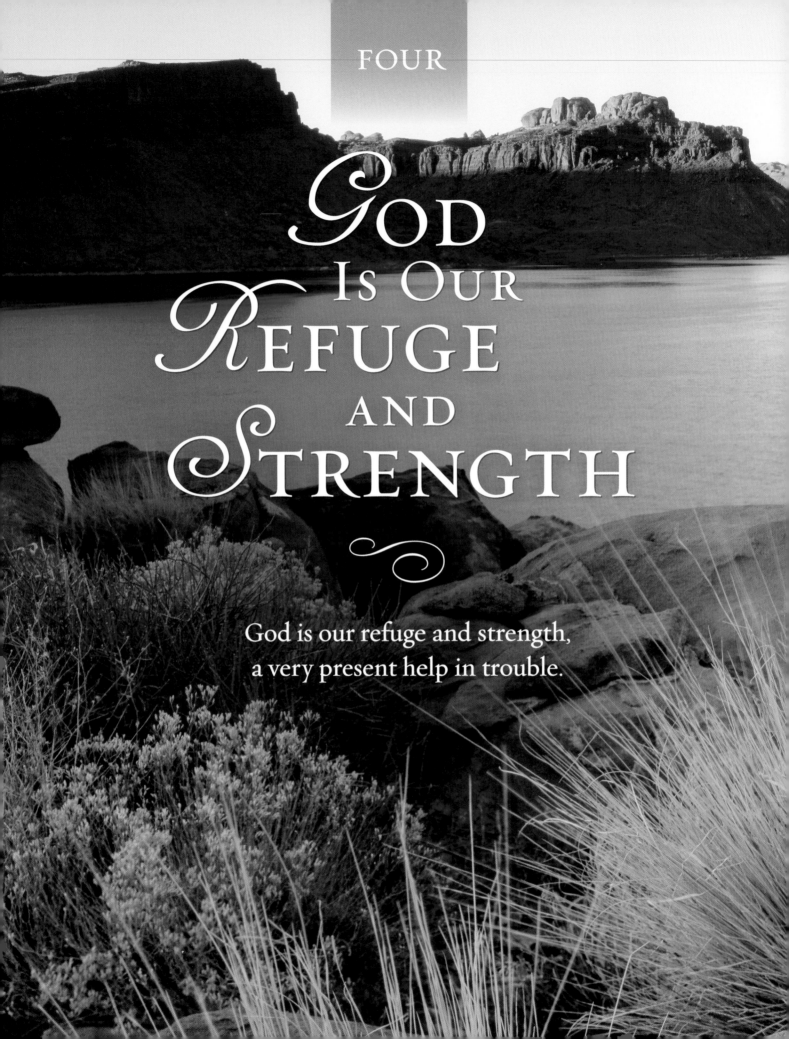

FOUR

GOD Is Our REFUGE AND STRENGTH

God is our refuge and strength,
a very present help in trouble.

PSALM 46

GOD IS OUR REFUGE AND STRENGTH, a very present help in trouble. Therefore will not we fear, though the earth be removed, and though the mountains be carried into the midst of the sea; Though the waters thereof roar and be troubled, though the mountains shake with the swelling thereof. Selah.

Be still, and know that I am God . . .

There is a river, the streams whereof shall make glad the city of God, the holy place of the tabernacles of the most High. God is in the midst of her; she shall not be moved: God shall help her, and that right early. The heathen raged, the kingdoms were moved: he uttered his voice, the earth melted. The LORD of hosts is with us; the God of Jacob is our refuge. Selah. Come, behold the works of the LORD, what desolations he hath made in the earth. He maketh wars to cease unto the end of the earth; he breaketh the bow, and cutteth the spear in sunder; he burneth the chariot in the fire.

Be still, and know that I am God: I will be exalted among the heathen, I will be exalted in the earth. The LORD of hosts is with us; the God of Jacob is our refuge. Selah.

Sandstone wall of Ottawa Canyon, Starved Rock State Park, Illinois.
Photograph by Terry Donnelly/Donnelly-Austin Photography

PSALM 18

I WILL LOVE THEE, O LORD, MY STRENGTH. The LORD is my rock, and my fortress, and my deliverer; my God, my strength, in whom I will trust; my buckler, and the horn of my salvation, and my high tower. I will call upon the LORD, who is worthy to be praised: so shall I be saved from mine enemies. . . .

He delivered me from my strong enemy, and from them which hated me: for they were too strong for me. They prevented me in the day of my calamity: but the LORD was my stay. He brought me

As for God, his way is perfect . . .

forth also into a large place; he delivered me, because he delighted in me. . . .

As for God, his way is perfect: the word of the LORD is tried: he is a buckler to all those that trust in him. For who is God save the LORD? or who is a rock save our God? It is God that girdeth me with strength, and maketh my way perfect. He maketh my feet like hinds' feet, and setteth me upon my high places. He teacheth my hands to war, so that a bow of steel is broken by mine arms. Thou hast also given me the shield of thy salvation: and thy right hand hath holden me up, and thy gentleness hath made me great. Thou hast enlarged my steps under me, that my feet did not slip. . . .

The LORD liveth; and blessed be my rock; and let the God of my salvation be exalted. It is God that avengeth me, and subdueth the people under me. He delivereth me from mine enemies: yea, thou liftest me up above those that rise up against me: thou hast delivered me from the violent man. Therefore will I give thanks unto thee, O LORD, among the heathen, and sing praises unto thy name. Great deliverance giveth he to his king; and sheweth mercy to his anointed, to David, and to his seed for evermore. (Verses 1–3, 17–19, 30–36, 46–50)

Magnolia blossoms at Arnold Arboretum in Boston, Massachussetts.
Photograph by William H. Johnson

A MIGHTY FORTRESS IS OUR GOD

Martin Luther, tr. by Frederick H. Hedge   Martin Luther

1. A might - y for - tress is our God, A
2. Did we in our own strength con - fide, Our
3. And tho' this world, with dev - ils filled, Should
4. That word a - bove all earth - ly pow'rs, No

bul - wark nev - er fail - ing;   Our
striv - ing would be los - ing,   Were
threat - en to un - do us,   We
thanks to them, a - bid - eth;   The

help - er He a - mid the flood Of mor - tal ills pre -
not the right man on our side, The man of God's own
will not fear, for God hath willed His truth to tri - umph
Spir - it and the gifts are ours Thro' Him who with us

PSALM 145

I WILL EXTOL THEE, MY GOD, O KING; and I will bless thy name for ever and ever. Every day will I bless thee; and I will praise thy name for ever and ever.

Great is the LORD, and greatly to be praised; and his greatness is unsearchable. One generation shall praise thy works to another, and shall declare thy mighty acts. I will speak of the glorious honour of thy majesty, and of thy wondrous works. And men shall speak of the might of thy terrible acts: and I will declare thy greatness. They shall abundantly utter the memory of thy great goodness, and shall sing of thy righteousness.

All thy works shall praise thee, O LORD …

The LORD is gracious, and full of compassion; slow to anger, and of great mercy. The LORD is good to all: and his tender mercies are over all his works. All thy works shall praise thee, O LORD; and thy saints shall bless thee. They shall speak of the glory of thy kingdom, and talk of thy power; To make known to the sons of men his mighty acts, and the glorious majesty of his kingdom. Thy kingdom is an everlasting kingdom, and thy dominion endureth throughout all generations. The LORD upholdeth all that fall, and raiseth up all those that be bowed down. The eyes of all wait upon thee; and thou givest them their meat in due season. Thou openest thine hand, and satisfiest the desire of every living thing. The LORD is righteous in all his ways, and holy in all his works. The LORD is nigh unto all them that call upon him, to all that call upon him in truth. He will fulfil the desire of them that fear him: he also will hear their cry, and will save them. The LORD preserveth all them that love him: but all the wicked will he destroy. My mouth shall speak the praise of the LORD: and let all flesh bless his holy name for ever and ever.

Moonrise over the Snake River and Teton Mountains in Grand Teton National Park, Wyoming. Photograph by Dennis Frates

PSALM 34

I WILL BLESS THE LORD AT ALL TIMES: his praise shall continually be in my mouth. My soul shall make her boast in the LORD: the humble shall hear thereof, and be glad. O magnify the LORD with me, and let us exalt his name together.

I sought the LORD, and he heard me, and delivered me from all my fears. They looked unto him, and were lightened: and their faces were not ashamed. This poor man cried, and the LORD heard him, and saved him out of all his troubles. The angel of the LORD encampeth round about them that fear him, and delivereth them.

The righteous cry, and the Lord heareth . . .

O taste and see that the LORD is good: blessed is the man that trusteth in him. O fear the LORD, ye his saints: for there is no want to them that fear him. The young lions do lack, and suffer hunger: but they that seek the LORD shall not want any good thing.

Come, ye children, hearken unto me: I will teach you the fear of the LORD. What man is he that desireth life, and loveth many days, that he may see good? Keep thy tongue from evil, and thy lips from speaking guile. Depart from evil, and do good; seek peace, and pursue it. The eyes of the LORD are upon the righteous, and his ears are open unto their cry. The face of the LORD is against them that do evil, to cut off the remembrance of them from the earth. The righteous cry, and the LORD heareth, and delivereth them out of all their troubles. The LORD is nigh unto them that are of a broken heart; and saveth such as be of a contrite spirit. Many are the afflictions of the righteous: but the LORD delivereth him out of them all.

(Verses 1–19)

Punchbowl Falls in Columbia River Gorge, Oregon. Photograph by Dennis Frates

O God, Our Help
(PSALM 90)

Isaac Watts

O God, our help in ages past,
Our hope for years to come,
Our shelter from the stormy blast,
And our eternal home:

Beneath the shadow of thy throne
Thy saints have dwelt secure;
Sufficient is thine arm alone,
And our defence is sure.

Before the hills in order stood
Or earth received her frame,
From everlasting thou art God,
To endless years the same.

A thousand ages in thy sight
Are like an evening gone,
Short as the watch that ends the night
Before the rising sun.

Time, like an ever-rolling stream,
Bears all its sons away;
They fly, forgotten, as a dream
Dies at the opening day.

Our God, our help in ages past,
Our hope for years to come,
Be thou our guard while troubles last,
And our eternal home!

The LORD is my strength and my shield; my heart trusted in him, and I am helped: therefore my heart greatly rejoiceth; and with my song will I praise him.

—PSALM 28:7

God Our Refuge

Richard C. Trench

If there had anywhere appeared in space
Another place of refuge where to flee,
Our hearts had taken refuge in that place
And not with thee.

For we against creation's bars had beat
Like prisoned eagles, through great world
    had sought
Though but a foot of ground to plant
    our feet,
Where thou were not.

And only when we found in earth and air,
In heaven or hell, that such might nowhere be—
That we could not flee from thee anywhere
We fled to thee.

The Place of Peace

Edwin Markham

At the heart of the cyclone tearing the sky
And flinging the clouds and the towers by,
Is a place of central calm;
So here in the roar of mortal things
I have a place where my spirit sings—
In the hollow of God's palm.

Eternal Assurance

Grace Noll Crowell

Throughout the ages men have clung
To the everlasting promises of God.
When loss and grief and suffering have wrung
Their hearts, the pilgrims journeying on earth's sod
Have turned their faces skyward and will turn
Forever toward the arching starlit skies,
Where steadfastly his silver fires burn
Like words of flame before their seeking eyes.

O men, behold!
Lift up your eyes and see
Who hath created them. He brings them out,
He names each one—he knows their destiny.
Not one will fail! Oh, we so prone to doubt,
Can we not trust the One through life's brief hour,
Who has such infinite, unfailing power?

Wings

Victor Hugo

Be like the bird
That, pausing in her flight
Awhile on boughs too slight,
Feels them give way
Beneath her and yet sings,
Knowing that she hath wings.

The Thought of God

Frederick Lucian Hosmer

One thought I have,
    my ample creed,
So deep it is and broad
And equal to my every need—
It is the thought of God.

Each morn unfolds
    some fresh surprise;
I feast at Life's full board;
And rising in my inner skies
Shines forth the thought of God.

At night my gladness is my prayer;
I drop my daily load;
And every care is pillowed there
Upon the thought of God.

PSALM *27*

THE LORD IS MY LIGHT AND MY SALVATION; whom shall I fear? the LORD is the strength of my life; of whom shall I be afraid? When the wicked, even mine enemies and my foes, came upon me to eat up my flesh, they stumbled and fell. Though an host should encamp against me, my heart shall not fear: though war should rise against me, in this will I be confident. One thing have I desired of the LORD, that will I seek after; that I may dwell in the

---

The LORD is my light and my salvation; whom shall I fear?

---

house of the LORD all the days of my life, to behold the beauty of the LORD, and to enquire in his temple. For in the time of trouble he shall hide me in his pavilion: in the secret of his tabernacle shall he hide me; he shall set me up upon a rock. And now shall mine head be lifted up above mine enemies round about me: therefore will I offer in his tabernacle sacrifices of joy; I will sing, yea, I will sing praises unto the LORD. Hear, O LORD, when I cry with my voice: have mercy also upon me, and answer me. When thou saidst, Seek ye my face; my heart said unto thee, Thy face, LORD, will I seek. Hide not thy face far from me; put not thy servant away in anger: thou hast been my help; leave me not, neither forsake me, O God of my salvation. When my father and my mother forsake me, then the LORD will take me up. Teach me thy way, O LORD, and lead me in a plain path, because of mine enemies. Deliver me not over unto the will of mine enemies: for false witnesses are risen up against me, and such as breathe out cruelty. I had fainted, unless I had believed to see the goodness of the LORD in the land of the living. Wait on the LORD: be of good courage, and he shall strengthen thine heart: wait, I say, on the LORD.

Sunset on Limahuli Beach, Kauai, Hawaii. Photograph by Dennis Frates

PSALM 40

I WAITED PATIENTLY FOR THE LORD; and he inclined unto me, and heard my cry. He brought me up also out of an horrible pit, out of the miry clay, and set my feet upon a rock, and established my goings. And he hath put a new song in my mouth, even praise unto our God: many shall see it, and fear, and shall trust in the LORD. Blessed is that man that maketh the LORD his trust, and respecteth not the proud, nor such as turn aside to lies.

Let all those that seek thee rejoice and be glad in thee. . . .

Many, O LORD my God, are thy wonderful works which thou hast done, and thy thoughts which are to us-ward: they cannot be reckoned up in order unto thee: if I would declare and speak of them, they are more than can be numbered. . . .

I have not hid thy righteousness within my heart; I have declared thy faithfulness and thy salvation: I have not concealed thy lovingkindness and thy truth from the great congregation. Withhold not thou thy tender mercies from me, O LORD: let thy lovingkindness and thy truth continually preserve me. For innumerable evils have compassed me about: mine iniquities have taken hold upon me, so that I am not able to look up; they are more than the hairs of mine head: therefore my heart faileth me. Be pleased, O LORD, to deliver me: O LORD, make haste to help me. . . .

Let all those that seek thee rejoice and be glad in thee: let such as love thy salvation say continually, The LORD be magnified. But I am poor and needy; yet the LORD thinketh upon me: thou art my help and my deliverer; make no tarrying, O my God.

(Verses 1–5, 10–13, 16–17)

Early snow dusting meadow in Grand Teton National Park, Wyoming.
Photograph by Terry Donnelly/Donnelly-Austin Photography

PSALM *118*

O GIVE THANKS UNTO THE LORD; for he is good: because his mercy endureth for ever. Let Israel now say, that his mercy endureth for ever. Let the house of Aaron now say, that his mercy endureth for ever. Let them now that fear the LORD say, that his mercy endureth for ever.

I called upon the LORD in distress: the LORD answered me, and set me in a large place. The LORD is on my side; I will not fear: what can man do unto me? The LORD taketh my part with them that help me: therefore shall I see my desire upon them that hate me.

The LORD is my strength and song . . .

It is better to trust in the LORD than to put confidence in man. It is better to trust in the LORD than to put confidence in princes. . . .

The LORD is my strength and song, and is become my salvation. The voice of rejoicing and salvation is in the tabernacles of the righteous: the right hand of the LORD doeth valiantly. The right hand of the LORD is exalted: the right hand of the LORD doeth valiantly. . . .

I will praise thee: for thou hast heard me, and art become my salvation. The stone which the builders refused is become the head stone of the corner. This is the LORD's doing; it is marvellous in our eyes.

This is the day which the LORD hath made; we will rejoice and be glad in it. Save now, I beseech thee, O LORD: O LORD, I beseech thee, send now prosperity.

Blessed be he that cometh in the name of the LORD: we have blessed you out of the house of the LORD.

Thou art my God, and I will praise thee: thou art my God, I will exalt thee. O give thanks unto the LORD; for he is good: for his mercy endureth for ever. (Verses 1–9, 14–16, 21–26, 28–29)

Fall leaves in Armstrong Creek, Starved Rock State Park, Illinois.
Photograph by Terry Donnelly/Donnelly-Austin Photography

PSALM 57

BE MERCIFUL UNTO ME, O GOD, be merciful unto me: for my soul trusteth in thee: yea, in the shadow of thy wings will I make my refuge, until these calamities be overpast. I will cry unto God most high; unto God that performeth all things for me. He shall send from heaven, and save me from the reproach of him that would swallow me up. Selah. God shall send forth his mercy and his truth.

In the shadow of thy wings will I make my refuge . . .

My soul is among lions: and I lie even among them that are set on fire, even the sons of men, whose teeth are spears and arrows, and their tongue a sharp sword.

Be thou exalted, O God, above the heavens; let thy glory be above all the earth.

They have prepared a net for my steps; my soul is bowed down: they have digged a pit before me, into the midst whereof they are fallen themselves. Selah.

My heart is fixed, O God, my heart is fixed: I will sing and give praise. Awake up, my glory; awake, psaltery and harp: I myself will awake early. I will praise thee, O LORD, among the people: I will sing unto thee among the nations. For thy mercy is great unto the heavens, and thy truth unto the clouds.

Be thou exalted, O God, above the heavens: let thy glory be above all the earth.

Sunrise at Secret Beach, Kauai, Hawaii. Photograph by Dennis Frates

Lines Written in Her Breviary

Saint Theresa, tr. by Henry Wadsworth Longfellow

Let nothing disturb thee,
Nothing affright thee;
All things are passing;
God never changeth;
Patient endurance
Attaineth to all things;
Who God possesseth
In nothing is wanting;
Alone God sufficeth.

Thy Presence

Henry Wadsworth Longfellow

The calmness bends serene above,
My restlessness to still;
Around me flows thy quickening life,
To nerve my faltering will;
Thy presence fills my solitude;
Thy providence turns all to good.

Light Shining Out of Darkness

William Cowper

God moves in a mysterious way
His wonders to perform;
He plants his footsteps in the sea
And rides upon the storm.

Deep in unfathomable mines
Of never-failing skill,
He treasures up his bright designs
And works his sovereign will.

Ye fearful saints, fresh courage take;
The clouds ye so much dread
Are big with mercy and shall break
In blessings on your head.

Judge not the Lord by feeble sense,
But trust him for his grace;
Behind a frowning providence
He hides a smiling face.

His purposes will ripen fast,
Unfolding every hour;
The bud may have a bitter taste,
But sweet will be the flower.

Blind unbelief is sure to err,
And scan his work in vain;
God is his own interpreter,
And he will make it plain.

Whom have I in heaven
but thee? and there is
none upon earth that I
desire beside thee.
My flesh and my heart faileth:
but God is the strength
of my heart, and
my portion for ever.

—PSALM 73:25–26

Our Burden Bearer

Phillips Brooks

The little sharp vexations
And the briars that cut the feet—
Why not take all to the Helper
Who has never failed us yet?
Tell him about the heartache,
And tell him the longings too;
Tell him the baffled purpose
When we scarce know what to do.
Then, leaving all our weakness
With the One divinely strong,
Forget that we bore the burden
And carry away the song.

I Know Not What the Future Hath

John Greenleaf Whittier

I know not what the future hath
Of marvel or surprise,
Assured alone that life and death
His mercy underlies.

And if my heart and flesh are weak
To bear an untried pain,
The bruised reed he will not break,
But strengthen and sustain.

No offering of my own I have,
Nor works my faith to prove;
I can but give the gifts he gave
And plead his love for love.

And so beside the silent sea
I wait the muffled oar;
No harm from him can come to me
On ocean or on shore.

I know not where his islands lift
Their fronded palms in air;
I only know I cannot drift
Beyond his love and care.

PSALM 91

HE THAT DWELLETH IN THE SECRET PLACE of the most High shall abide under the shadow of the Almighty. I will say of the LORD, He is my refuge and my fortress: my God; in him will I trust. Surely he shall deliver thee from the snare of the fowler, and from the noisome pestilence. He shall cover thee with his feathers, and under his wings shalt thou trust: his truth shall be thy shield and buckler. Thou shalt not be afraid for the terror by night; nor for the arrow that

I will say of the LORD, He is my refuge and my fortress . . .

flieth by day; Nor for the pestilence that walketh in darkness; nor for the destruction that wasteth at noonday. A thousand shall fall at thy side, and ten thousand at thy right hand; but it shall not come nigh thee. Only with thine eyes shalt thou behold and see the reward of the wicked. Because thou hast made the LORD, which is my refuge, even the most High, thy habitation; There shall no evil befall thee, neither shall any plague come nigh thy dwelling. For he shall give his angels charge over thee, to keep thee in all thy ways. They shall bear thee up in their hands, lest thou dash thy foot against a stone. Thou shalt tread upon the lion and adder: the young lion and the dragon shalt thou trample under feet. Because he hath set his love upon me, therefore will I deliver him: I will set him on high, because he hath known my name. He shall call upon me, and I will answer him: I will be with him in trouble; I will deliver him, and honour him. With long life will I satisfy him, and shew him my salvation.

Fireweed blossoms along Nuka Bay in Kenai Fjords National Park, Alaska. Photograph by Carr Clifton

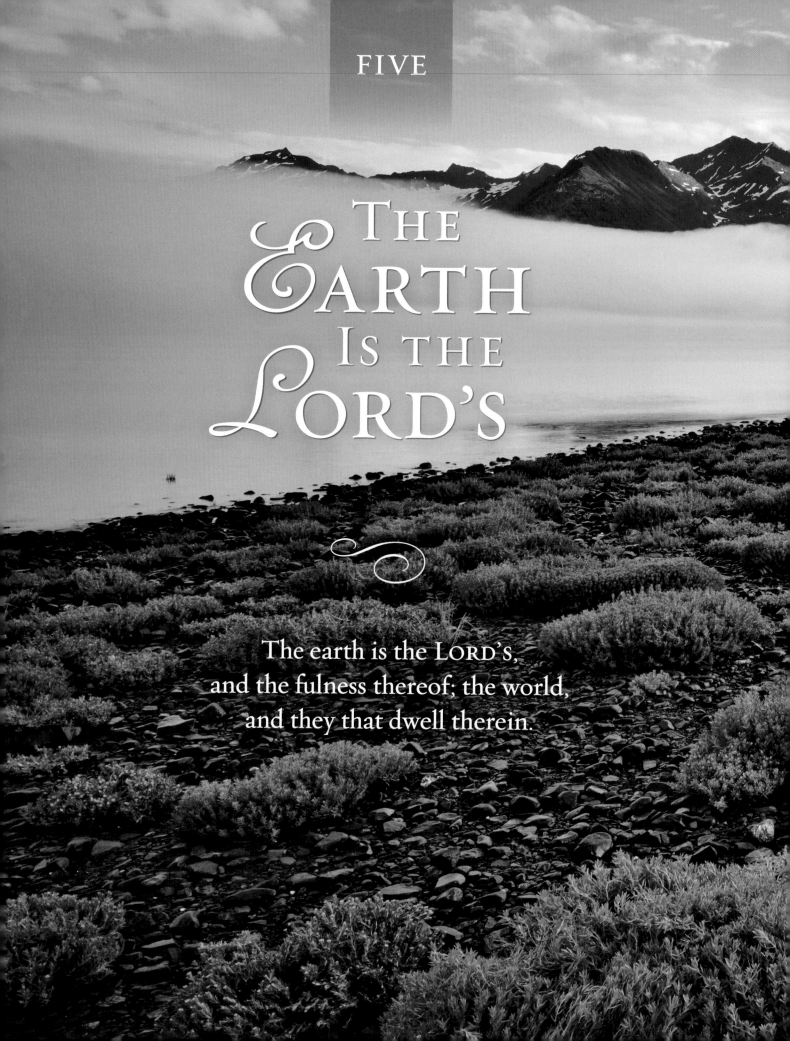

FIVE

THE EARTH IS THE LORD'S

The earth is the LORD's,
and the fulness thereof; the world,
and they that dwell therein.

PSALM 24

THE EARTH IS THE LORD'S, and the fulness thereof; the world, and they that dwell therein. For he hath founded it upon the seas, and established it upon the floods. Who shall ascend into the hill of the LORD? or who shall stand in his holy place? He that hath clean hands, and a pure heart; who hath not lifted up his soul unto vanity, nor sworn deceitfully. He shall receive the blessing

---

> Who shall ascend into the
> hill of the LORD? or who shall
> stand in his holy place?
> He that hath clean hands,
> and a pure heart . . .

---

from the LORD, and righteousness from the God of his salvation. This is the generation of them that seek him, that seek thy face, O Jacob. Selah.

Lift up your heads, O ye gates; and be ye lift up, ye everlasting doors; and the King of glory shall come in. Who is this King of glory? The LORD strong and mighty, the LORD mighty in battle. Lift up your heads, O ye gates; even lift them up, ye everlasting doors; and the King of glory shall come in. Who is this King of glory? The LORD of hosts, he is the King of glory. Selah.

False Hellebore in Allegany State Park, New York.
Photograph by Carr Clifton

The day is thine, the night also is thine:
thou hast prepared the light and the sun.
Thou hast set all the borders of the earth:
thou hast made summer and winter.

—PSALM 74:16–17

Ode

Joseph Addison

The spacious firmament on high,
With all the blue ethereal sky,
And spangled heavens, a shining frame,
Their great Original proclaim.
The unwearied sun, from day to day,
Does his Creator's power display,
And publishes to every land
The work of an Almighty hand.

Soon as the evening shades prevail,
The moon takes up the wondrous tale,
And nightly to the listening earth
Repeats the story of her birth;

Whilst all the stars that round her burn
And all the planets, in their turn,
Confirm the tidings as they roll
And spread the truth from pole to pole.

What though, in solemn silence, all
Move round the dark terrestrial ball;
What though no real voice or sound
Amidst their radiant orbs be found:
In reason's ear they all rejoice
And utter forth a glorious voice,
Forever singing as they shine,
"The hand that made us is divine."

God's Grandeur

Gerard Manley Hopkins

The world is charged with the grandeur
  of God.
It will flame out, like shining from shook foil;
It gathers to a greatness, like the ooze of oil
Crushed. Why do men then now not reck
  his rod?
Generations have trod, have trod, have trod;
And all is seared with trade; bleared, smeared
  with toil;
And wears man's smudge and shares
  man's smell: the soil
Is bare now, nor can foot feel, being shod.

And for all this, nature is never spent;
There lives the dearest freshness deep
  down things;
And though the last lights off the black
  West went
Oh, morning, at the brown brink
  eastward, springs—
Because the Holy Ghost over the bent
World broods with warm breast and with ah!
  bright wings.

God of the Earth, the Sky, the Sea

Samuel Longfellow

God of the earth, the sky, the sea,
Maker of all above, below,
Creation lives and moves in thee;
Thy present life through all doth flow.

Thy love is in the sunshine's glow;
Thy life is in the quickening air;
When lightnings flash and storm winds blow,
There is thy power; thy law is there.

We feel thy calm at evening's hour,
Thy grandeur in the march of night,
And when the morning breaks in power,
We hear thy word, "Let there be light."

But higher far, and far more clear,
Thee in man's spirit we behold;
Thine image and thyself are there—
Th' indwelling God, proclaimed of old.

PSALM 8

O LORD, OUR LORD, how excellent is thy name in all the earth! who hast set thy glory above the heavens.

Out of the mouth of babes and sucklings hast thou ordained strength because of thine enemies, that thou mightest still the enemy and the avenger.

When I consider thy heavens, the work of thy fingers, the moon and the stars, which thou hast

What is man, that thou art mindful of him?

ordained; What is man, that thou art mindful of him? and the son of man, that thou visitest him? For thou hast made him a little lower than the angels, and hast crowned him with glory and honour. Thou madest him to have dominion over the works of thy hands; thou hast put all things under his feet: All sheep and oxen, yea, and the beasts of the field; The fowl of the air, and the fish of the sea, and whatsoever passeth through the paths of the seas.

O LORD our LORD, how excellent is thy name in all the earth!

Full moon over the Grand Canyon at sunset as seen from Pima Point, Grand Canyon National Park, Arizona. Photograph by Tim Fitzharris/Minden Pictures

ALL THINGS BRIGHT AND BEAUTIFUL

Cecil Frances Alexander   English melody

All things bright and beau - ti - ful, All crea - tures great and

small.   All things wise and

won - der - ful: The Lord God made them all.

PSALM 19

THE HEAVENS DECLARE THE GLORY OF GOD; and the firmament sheweth his handywork. Day unto day uttereth speech, and night unto night sheweth knowledge. There is no speech nor language, where their voice is not heard. Their line is gone out through all the earth, and their words to the end of the world. In them hath he set a tabernacle for the sun, Which is as a bridegroom coming out of

The law of the LORD is perfect, converting the soul . . .

his chamber, and rejoiceth as a strong man to run a race. His going forth is from the end of the heaven, and his circuit unto the ends of it: and there is nothing hid from the heat thereof.

The law of the LORD is perfect, converting the soul: the testimony of the LORD is sure, making wise the simple. The statutes of the LORD are right, rejoicing the heart: the commandment of the LORD is pure, enlightening the eyes. The fear of the LORD is clean, enduring for ever: the judgments of the LORD are true and righteous altogether. More to be desired are they than gold, yea, than much fine gold: sweeter also than honey and the honeycomb. Moreover by them is thy servant warned: and in keeping of them there is great reward. Who can understand his errors? cleanse thou me from secret faults. Keep back thy servant also from presumptuous sins; let them not have dominion over me: then shall I be upright, and I shall be innocent from the great transgression. Let the words of my mouth, and the meditation of my heart, be acceptable in thy sight, O LORD, my strength, and my redeemer.

The Napali Coast on Kauai, Hawaii. Photograph by Dennis Frates

PSALM 104

BLESS THE LORD, O MY SOUL. O LORD my God, thou art very great; thou art clothed with honour and majesty. Who coverest thyself with light as with a garment: who stretchest out the heavens like a curtain: Who layeth the beams of his chambers in the waters: who maketh the clouds his chariot: who walketh upon the wings of the wind: Who maketh his angels spirits; his ministers a flaming fire: Who laid the foundations of the earth, that it should not be removed for ever.

He sendeth the springs into the valleys, which run among the hills.

Thou coveredst it with the deep as with a garment: the waters stood above the mountains. At thy rebuke they fled; at the voice of thy thunder they hasted away. They go up by the mountains; they go down by the valleys unto the place which thou hast founded for them. Thou hast set a bound that they may not pass over; that they turn not again to cover the earth.

He sendeth the springs into the valleys, which run among the hills. They give drink to every beast of the field: the wild asses quench their thirst. By them shall the fowls of the heaven have their habitation, which sing among the branches. He watereth the hills from his chambers: the earth is satisfied with the fruit of thy works. . . .

I will sing unto the LORD as long as I live: I will sing praise to my God while I have my being. My meditation of him shall be sweet: I will be glad in the LORD. Let the sinners be consumed out of the earth, and let the wicked be no more. Bless thou the LORD, O my soul. Praise ye the LORD. (Verses 1–13, 33–35)

Balsam root and lupine in the Columbia Gorge National Scenic Area, Oregon.
Photograph by Terry Donnelly/Donnelly-Austin Photography

PSALM 72

GIVE THE KING THY JUDGMENTS, O God, and thy righteousness unto the king's son. He shall judge thy people with righteousness, and thy poor with judgment.

The mountains shall bring peace to the people, and the little hills, by righteousness. He shall judge the poor of the people, he shall save the children of the needy, and shall break in pieces the oppressor. They shall fear thee as long as the sun and moon endure, throughout all generations.

His name shall be continued as long as the sun. . .

He shall come down like rain upon the mown grass: as showers that water the earth. In his days shall the righteous flourish; and abundance of peace so long as the moon endureth. He shall have dominion also from sea to sea, and from the river unto the ends of the earth. . . .

For he shall deliver the needy when he crieth; the poor also, and him that hath no helper. He shall spare the poor and needy, and shall save the souls of the needy. He shall redeem their soul from deceit and violence: and precious shall their blood be in his sight. . . .

His name shall endure for ever: his name shall be continued as long as the sun: and men shall be blessed in him: all nations shall call him blessed. Blessed be the LORD God, the God of Israel, who only doeth wondrous things.

And blessed be his glorious name for ever: and let the whole earth be filled with his glory; Amen, and Amen.

(Verses 1–8, 12–14, 17–19)

Photograph © Corbis

Pied Beauty

Gerard Manley Hopkins

Glory be to God for dappled things—
For skies of couple-colour as a brinded cow;
For rose-moles all in stipple upon trout that swim;
Fresh-firecoal chestnut-falls; finches' wings;
Landscape plotted and pieced—fold, fallow, and plow;
And all trades, their gear and tackle and trim.

All things counter, original, spare, strange;
Whatever is fickle, freckled (who knows how?)
With swift, slow; sweet, sour; adazzle, dim;
He fathers-forth whose beauty is past change:
    Praise him.

Out of the Vast

Augustus Wright Bamberger

There's a part of the sun in the apple;
There's a part of the moon in a rose;
There's a part of the flaming Pleiades
In every leaf that grows.

Out of the vast comes nearness;
For the God whose love we sing
Lends a little of his heaven
To every living thing.

Jesus Shall Reign Where'er the Sun

Isaac Watts

Jesus shall reign where'er the sun
Does his successive journeys run;
His kingdom stretch from shore to shore
Till moon shall wax and wane no more.

To him shall endless prayer be made
And praises throng to crown his head;
His name, like sweet perfume, shall rise
With every morning sacrifice.

People and realms of every tongue
Dwell on his love with sweetest song,

And infant voices shall proclaim
Their early blessings on his name.

Blessings abound where'er he reigns;
The prisoner leaps to loose his chains;
The weary find eternal rest,
And all the sons of want are blest.

Let every creature rise and bring
Peculiar honors to our King;
Angels descend with songs again,
And earth repeat the loud Amen!

This Is My Father's World

Maltbie D. Babcock

This is my Father's world, and to my listening ears
All nature sings, and round me rings the music of the spheres.
This is my Father's world: I rest me in the thought
Of rocks and trees, of skies and seas;
His hand the wonders wrought.

This is my Father's world, the birds their carols raise,
The morning light, the lily white, declare their Maker's praise.
This is my Father's world: he shines in all that's fair;
In the rustling grass I hear him pass;
He speaks to me everywhere.

This is my Father's world. O let me ne'er forget
That though the wrong seems oft so strong, God is the ruler yet.
This is my Father's world: the battle is not done;
Jesus who died shall be satisfied,
And earth and heaven be one.

O give thanks unto the LORD; for he is good:
for his mercy endureth for ever. . . .
To him that stretched out the earth above the waters:
for his mercy endureth for ever.

—PSALM 136:1, 6

SIX

GREAT IS THE LORD

Great is the LORD, and greatly
to be praised in the city of our God,
in the mountain of his holiness.

PSALM 48

GREAT IS THE LORD, and greatly to be praised in the city of our God, in the mountain of his holiness. Beautiful for situation, the joy of the whole earth, is mount Zion, on the sides of the north, the city of the great King. God is known in her palaces for a refuge. For, lo, the kings were assembled, they passed by together. They saw it, and so they marvelled; they were troubled, and hasted away. Fear took hold upon

Great is the LORD, and greatly to be praised . . .

them there, and pain, as of a woman in travail. Thou breakest the ships of Tarshish with an east wind. As we have heard, so have we seen in the city of the LORD of hosts, in the city of our God: God will establish it for ever. Selah.

We have thought of thy lovingkindness, O God, in the midst of thy temple. According to thy name, O God, so is thy praise unto the ends of the earth: thy right hand is full of righteousness. Let mount Zion rejoice, let the daughters of Judah be glad, because of thy judgments. Walk about Zion, and go round about her: tell the towers thereof. Mark ye well her bulwarks, consider her palaces; that ye may tell it to the generation following. For this God is our God for ever and ever: he will be our guide even unto death.

Sitka Spruce forest, Shuyak Island State Park, Alaska. Photograph by Carr Clifton

PSALM *93*

THE LORD REIGNETH, he is clothed with majesty; the LORD is clothed with strength, wherewith he hath girded himself: the world also is stablished, that it cannot be moved.

The LORD on high
is mightier than the noise
of many waters, yea, than
the mighty waves of the sea.

Thy throne is established of old: thou art from everlasting. The floods have lifted up, O LORD, the floods have lifted up their voice; the floods lift up their waves.

The LORD on high is mightier than the noise of many waters, yea, than the mighty waves of the sea. Thy testimonies are very sure: holiness becometh thine house, O LORD, for ever.

Sunset on Napali Coast on Kauai, Hawaii. Photograph by Dennis Frates

Praise to the Holiest

John Henry Newman

Praise to the Holiest in the height,
And in the depth be praise;
In all his words most wonderful,
Most sure in all his ways. . . .

O loving wisdom of our God!
When all was sin and shame,
A second Adam to the fight
And to the rescue came.

O wisest love! that flesh and blood,
Which did in Adam fail,
Should strive afresh against the foe,
Should strive and should prevail.

And that a higher gift than grace
Should flesh and blood refine;

God's presence and his very self,
And essence all-divine.

O generous love! Thee who smote
In man, for man, the foe,
The double agony in man,
For man, should undergo.

And in the garden secretly,
And on the cross on high
Should teach his brethren and inspire
To suffer and to die.

Praise to the Holiest in the height,
And in the depths be praise;
In all his words most wonderful,
Most sure in all his ways.

LORD, thou hast been our dwelling place in all generations. Before the mountains were brought forth, or ever thou hadst formed the earth and the world, even from everlasting to everlasting, thou art God.

—PSALM 90:1–2

Father, How Wide Thy Glories Shine

Charles Wesley

Father, how wide thy glories shine,
God of the universe and mine!
Thy goodness watches o'er the whole,
As all mankind were but one soul,
Yet keeps my every sacred hair,
As I remain'd thy single care.

A Sun-Day Hymn

Oliver Wendell Holmes

Lord of all being, throned afar,
Thy glory flames from sun and star;
Center and soul of every sphere,
Yet to each loving heart how near!

Sun of our life, thy quickening ray
Sheds on our path the glow of day:
Star of our hope, thy softened light
Cheers the long watches of the night.

Our midnight is thy smile withdrawn;
Our noontide is thy gracious dawn;

Our rainbow arch, thy mercy's sign:
All, save the clouds of sin, are thine.

Lord of all life, below, above,
Whose light is truth, whose warmth is love,
Before thy ever-blazing throne
We ask no luster of our own.

Grant us thy truth to make us free,
And kindling hearts that burn for thee,
Till all thy living altars claim
One holy light, one heavenly flame.

Sheer Joy

Ralph Spaulding Cushman

Oh the sheer joy of it!
Living with thee,
God of the universe,
Lord of a tree,
Maker of mountains,
Lover of me!

Oh the sheer joy of it!
Breathing thy air,
Morning is dawning,
Gone every care.

All the world's singing,
"God's everywhere."

Oh the sheer joy of it!
Walking with thee
Out on the hilltop,
Down by the sea.
Life is so wonderful;
Life is so free.

Oh the sheer joy of it!
Working with God,

Running his errands,
Waiting his nod,
Building his heaven
On common sod.

Oh the sheer joy of it!
Ever to be
Living in glory,
Living with thee,
Lord of tomorrow,
Lover of me!

PSALM 111

PRAISE YE THE LORD. I will praise the LORD with my whole heart, in the assembly of the upright, and in the congregation. The works of the LORD are great, sought out of all them that have pleasure therein. His work is honourable and glorious: and his righteousness endureth for ever. He hath made his wonderful works to be remembered: the

The fear of the LORD is the beginning of wisdom . . .

LORD is gracious and full of compassion. He hath given meat unto them that fear him: he will ever be mindful of his covenant. He hath shewed his people the power of his works, that he may give them the heritage of the heathen. The works of his hands are verity and judgment; all his commandments are sure. They stand fast for ever and ever, and are done in truth and uprightness. He sent redemption unto his people: he hath commanded his covenant for ever: holy and reverend is his name. The fear of the LORD is the beginning of wisdom: a good understanding have all they that do his commandments: his praise endureth for ever.

Lichen patterns on boulder and reflections in Beaver Pond, White Mountain National Forest, New Hampshire. Photograph by Carr Clifton

PSALM *147*

PRAISE YE THE LORD: for it is good to sing praises unto our God; for it is pleasant; and praise is comely.

The LORD doth build up Jerusalem: he gathereth together the outcasts of Israel. He healeth the broken in heart, and bindeth up their wounds. He telleth the number of the stars; he calleth them all by their names.

Great is our LORD, and of great power: his understanding is infinite. The LORD lifteth up the meek: he casteth the wicked down to the ground.

Sing unto the LORD with thanksgiving . . .

Sing unto the LORD with thanksgiving; sing praise upon the harp unto our God: Who covereth the heaven with clouds, who prepareth rain for the earth, who maketh grass to grow upon the mountains. He giveth to the beast his food, and to the young ravens which cry. He delighteth not in the strength of the horse: he taketh not pleasure in the legs of a man. The LORD taketh pleasure in them that fear him, in those that hope in his mercy.

Praise the LORD, O Jerusalem; praise thy God, O Zion. For he hath strengthened the bars of thy gates; he hath blessed thy children within thee. He maketh peace in thy borders, and filleth thee with the finest of the wheat. He sendeth forth his commandment upon earth: his word runneth very swiftly. He giveth snow like wool: he scattereth the hoarfrost like ashes. He casteth forth his ice like morsels: who can stand before his cold? He sendeth out his word, and melteth them: he causeth his wind to blow, and the waters flow. He sheweth his word unto Jacob, his statutes and his judgments unto Israel. He hath not dealt so with any nation: and as for his judgments, they have not known them. Praise ye the LORD.

*The Popo Agie River, Popo Agie Wilderness, Shoshone
National Forest, Wyoming. Photograph by Carr Clifton*

HOW GREAT THOU ART

Stuart K. Hine   *Stuart K. Hine*

1. O Lord, my God, when I in awe-some
2. When thro' the woods and for-est glades I
3. And when I think that God, His Son not
4. When Christ shall come with shout of ac-cla-

won-der Con-sid-er all the worlds Thy hands have
wan-der And hear the birds sing sweet-ly in the
spar-ing, Sent Him to die, I scarce can take it
ma-tion And take me home, what joy shall fill my

made, I see the stars, I hear the roll-ing
trees, When I look down from loft-y moun-tain
in; That on the cross, my bur-den glad-ly
heart! Then I shall bow in hum-ble ad-o-

thun- der, Thy pow'r thro' - out   the u - ni - verse dis - played.
gran- deur, And hear the   brook   and feel the gen - tle   breeze;
bear - ing, He bled and   died   to take a - way my   sin.
ra - tion And there pro - claim: my God, how great Thou   art!

Then sings my soul,   my Sav - ior God, to   Thee;   How great Thou

art! How great Thou   art! Then sings my   soul,   my Sav - ior God, to

Thee;   How great Thou   art! How great Thou   art!

PSALM *113*

PRAISE YE THE LORD. Praise, O ye servants of the LORD, praise the name of the LORD.

Blessed be the name of the LORD from this time forth and for evermore. From the rising of the sun unto the going down of the same the LORD's name is to be praised. The LORD is high above all nations, and his glory above the heavens.

Blessed be the name of the LORD from this time forth and for evermore.

Who is like unto the LORD our God, who dwelleth on high, Who humbleth himself to behold the things that are in heaven, and in the earth! He raiseth up the poor out of the dust, and lifteth the needy out of the dunghill; That he may set him with princes, even with the princes of his people. He maketh the barren woman to keep house, and to be a joyful mother of children. Praise ye the LORD.

Bluff-top view of forest near Lake of the Clouds in Porcupine Mountains Wilderness State Park, Michigan. Photograph by Terry Donnelly/Donnelly-Austin Photography

PSALM 146

PRAISE YE THE LORD. Praise the LORD, O my soul. While I live will I praise the Lord: I will sing praises unto my God while I have any being.

Put not your trust in princes, nor in the son of man, in whom there is no help. His breath goeth forth, he returneth to his earth; in that very day his thoughts perish.

The LORD openeth the eyes of the blind: the LORD raiseth them that are bowed down. . . .

Happy is he that hath the God of Jacob for his help, whose hope is in the LORD his God: Which made heaven, and earth, the sea, and all that therein is: which keepeth truth for ever: Which executeth judgment for the oppressed: which giveth food to the hungry. The LORD looseth the prisoners: The LORD openeth the eyes of the blind: the LORD raiseth them that are bowed down: the LORD loveth the righteous: The LORD preserveth the strangers; he relieveth the fatherless and widow: but the way of the wicked he turneth upside down.

The LORD shall reign for ever, even thy God, O Zion, unto all generations. Praise ye the LORD.

Sunrise in Blackstone Bay, Prince William Sound, Chugach National Forest, Alaska. Photograph by Carr Clifton

Let Us, with a Gladsome Mind

John Milton

Let us, with a gladsome mind,
Praise the Lord, for he is kind.
For his mercies aye endure,
Ever faithful, ever sure.

Let us blaze his name abroad,
For of gods he is the God; . . .
Who by all-commanding might
Filled the new-made world with light.

He the golden tressèd sun
Caused all day his course to run;

Th' horned moon to shine by night,
'Mid her spangled sisters bright.

He his chosen race did bless,
In the wasteful wilderness;
He hath, with a piteous eye,
Looked upon our misery.

All things living he doth feed.
His full hand supplies their need;
For his mercies aye endure,
Ever faithful, ever sure.

Great Art Thou, O Lord

Saint Augustine

Great art thou, O Lord, and greatly to be praised;
Great is thy power, and of thy wisdom there is no end.
And man, being a part of thy creation,
    desires to praise thee—
Man, who bears about him his mortality,
The witness of his sin, even the witness that
    thou "resistest the proud."
Yet man, this part of thy creation, desires to praise thee.
Thou movest us to delight in praising thee,
For thou hast formed us for thyself,
And our hearts are restless till they find rest in thee.

Blessed be the
LORD God of Israel
from everlasting, and
to everlasting. Amen,
and Amen.

—PSALM 41:13

Holy, Holy, Holy

Reginald Heber

Holy, holy, holy! Lord God Almighty!
Early in the morning our song shall
   rise to thee;
Holy, holy, holy! Merciful and mighty!
God in three Persons, blessèd Trinity!

Holy, holy, holy! All the saints adore thee,
Casting down their golden crowns around
   the glassy sea;
Cherubim and seraphim falling down before thee,
Which wert, and art, and evermore shalt be.

Holy, holy, holy! Though the darkness hide thee,
Though the eye of sinful man thy glory
   may not see,
Only thou art holy; there is none beside thee,
Perfect in power, in love, and purity.

Holy, holy, holy! Lord God Almighty!
All thy works shall praise thy name, in earth,
   and sky, and sea;
Holy, holy, holy! Merciful and mighty!
God in three Persons, blessèd Trinity!

All People That on Earth Do Dwell

William Kethe

All people that on earth do dwell,
Sing to the Lord with cheerful voice;
Him serve with mirth, his praise
   forth tell,
Come ye before him and rejoice.

Know that the Lord is God indeed;
Without our aid he did us make;
We are his folk; he doth us feed;
And for his sheep he doth us take.

Oh, enter then his gates with praise,
Approach with joy his courts unto;
Praise, laud, and bless his name always,
For it is seemly so to do.

For why? The Lord our God is good,
His mercy is forever sure;
His truth at all times firmly stood,
And shall from age to age endure.

PSALM 89

I WILL SING OF THE MERCIES OF THE LORD FOR EVER: with my mouth will I make known thy faithfulness to all generations. For I have said, Mercy shall be built up for ever: thy faithfulness shalt thou establish in the very heavens. I have made a covenant with my chosen, I have sworn unto David my servant, Thy seed will I establish for ever, and build up thy throne to all generations. Selah. And the heavens shall praise thy wonders, O LORD: thy faithfulness also in the congregation of the saints. For who in the heaven can

I will sing of the mercies of the LORD for ever . . .

be compared unto the LORD? who among the sons of the mighty can be likened unto the LORD? God is greatly to be feared in the assembly of the saints, and to be had in reverence of all them that are about him.

O LORD God of hosts, who is a strong LORD like unto thee? or to thy faithfulness round about thee? Thou rulest the raging of the sea: when the waves thereof arise, thou stillest them. Thou hast broken Rahab in pieces, as one that is slain; thou hast scattered thine enemies with thy strong arm. The heavens are thine, the earth also is thine: as for the world and the fulness thereof, thou hast founded them. The north and the south thou hast created them: Tabor and Hermon shall rejoice in thy name. Thou hast a mighty arm: strong is thy hand, and high is thy right hand. Justice and judgment are the habitation of thy throne: mercy and truth shall go before thy face. Blessed is the people that know the joyful sound: they shall walk, O LORD, in the light of thy countenance. In thy name shall they rejoice all the day: and in thy righteousness shall they be exalted. (VERSES 1–16)

Trees surrounded by mist in Yosemite National Park, California.
Photograph © age fotostock/SuperStock

PSALM *103*

BLESS THE LORD, O MY SOUL: and all that is within me, bless his holy name. Bless the LORD, O my soul, and forget not all his benefits: Who forgiveth all thine iniquities; who healeth all thy diseases; Who redeemeth thy life from destruction; who crowneth thee with lovingkindness and tender mercies; . . .

The LORD is merciful and gracious, slow to anger, and plenteous in mercy. He will not always chide: neither will he keep

---

The LORD is merciful and gracious, slow to anger, and plenteous in mercy.

---

his anger for ever. He hath not dealt with us after our sins; nor rewarded us according to our iniquities. For as the heaven is high above the earth, so great is his mercy toward them that fear him. As far as the east is from the west, so far hath he removed our transgressions from us. Like as a father pitieth his children, so the LORD pitieth them that fear him. For he knoweth our frame; he remembereth that we are dust. As for man, his days are as grass: as a flower of the field, so he flourisheth. For the wind passeth over it, and it is gone; and the place thereof shall know it no more.

But the mercy of the LORD is from everlasting to everlasting upon them that fear him, and his righteousness unto children's children; To such as keep his covenant, and to those that remember his commandments to do them. The LORD hath prepared his throne in the heavens; and his kingdom ruleth over all.

Bless the LORD, ye his angels, that excel in strength, that do his commandments, hearkening unto the voice of his word. Bless ye the Lord, all ye his hosts; ye ministers of his, that do his pleasure. Bless the Lord, all his works in all places of his dominion: bless the Lord, O my soul. (VERSES 1–4, 8–22)

Photograph © Cusp/SuperStock

SEVEN

SING UNTO THE LORD A NEW SONG

O sing unto the LORD a new song:
sing unto the LORD, all the earth.

PSALM 96

O SING UNTO THE LORD A NEW SONG: sing unto the LORD, all the earth. Sing unto the LORD, bless his name; shew forth his salvation from day to day. Declare his glory among the heathen, his wonders among all people. For the LORD is great, and greatly to be praised: he is to be feared above all gods. For all the gods of the nations are idols: but the LORD made the heavens. Honour and majesty are before him: strength and beauty are in his sanctuary.

> ## Give unto the LORD, O ye kindreds of the people, give unto the LORD glory and strength.

Give unto the LORD, O ye kindreds of the people, give unto the LORD glory and strength. Give unto the LORD the glory due unto his name: bring an offering, and come into his courts. O worship the LORD in the beauty of holiness: fear before him, all the earth. Say among the heathen that the LORD reigneth: the world also shall be established that it shall not be moved: he shall judge the people righteously.

Let the heavens rejoice, and let the earth be glad; let the sea roar, and the fulness thereof. Let the field be joyful, and all that is therein: then shall all the trees of the wood rejoice Before the LORD: for he cometh, for he cometh to judge the earth: he shall judge the world with righteousness, and the people with his truth.

Saguaro cactus in a field of Mexican gold poppies in Organ Pipe Cactus National Monument, Arizona, in view of the Ajo Mountains.
Photograph by Terry Donnelly/Donnelly-Austin Photography

PSALM *108*

O GOD, MY HEART IS FIXED; I will sing and give praise, even with my glory. Awake, psaltery and harp: I myself will awake early.

I will praise thee, O LORD, among the people: and I will sing praises unto thee among the nations. For thy mercy is great above the heavens: and thy truth reacheth unto the clouds.

For thy mercy is great above the heavens: and thy truth reacheth unto the clouds.

Be thou exalted, O God, above the heavens: and thy glory above all the earth;

That thy beloved may be delivered: save with thy right hand, and answer me. (VERSES 1–6)

Lake Superior, Pictured Rocks National Lakeshore, Michigan.
Photograph by Carr Clifton

JOYFUL, JOYFUL WE ADORE THEE

Henry van Dyke

Arranged from Ludwig van Beethoven by Edward Hodges

1. Joy - ful, joy - ful, we a - dore Thee,
2. All Thy works with joy sur - round Thee,
3. Thou art giv - ing and for - giv - ing,
4. Mor - tals, join the might - y cho - rus

God of glo - ry, Lord of love;
Earth and heav'n re - flect Thy rays.
Ev - er bless - ing, ev - er blest,
Which the morn - ing stars be - gan;

Hearts un - fold like flow'rs be - fore Thee,
Stars and an - gels sing a - round Thee,
Well - spring of the joy of liv - ing,
Love di - vine is reign - ing o'er us,

Open - ing to the sun a - bove.
Cen - ter of un - bro - ken praise.
O - cean depth of hap - py rest!
Lead - ing us with mer - cy's hand.

Melt the clouds of sin and sad - ness;
Field and for - est, vale and moun - tain,
Thou our Fa - ther, Christ our Broth - er,
Ev - er sing - ing, march we on - ward,

Drive the dark of doubt a - way. Giv - er of im -
Flow - ery mead - ow, flash - ing sea, Chant-ing bird and
All who live in love are Thine. Teach us how to
Vic - tors in the midst of strife. Joy - ful mu - sic

mor - tal glad - ness, Fill us with the light of day!
flow - ing foun - tain Call us to re - joice in Thee!
love each oth - er; Lift us to the joy di - vine!
leads us sun - ward In the tri - umph song of life!

PSALM 33

REJOICE IN THE LORD, O YE RIGHTEOUS: for praise is comely for the upright. Praise the LORD with harp: sing unto him with the psaltery and an instrument of ten strings. Sing unto him a new song; play skilfully with a loud noise. For the word of the LORD is right; and all his works are done in truth. He loveth righteousness and judgment: the earth is full of the goodness of the LORD. By the word of the LORD were the heavens made; and all the host of them by the breath of his mouth. He gathereth the waters of

---

Blessed is the nation whose God is the LORD . . .

---

the sea together as an heap: he layeth up the depth in storehouses. Let all the earth fear the LORD: let all the inhabitants of the world stand in awe of him. For he spake, and it was done; he commanded, and it stood fast. The LORD bringeth the counsel of the heathen to nought: he maketh the devices of the people of none effect. The counsel of the LORD standeth for ever, the thoughts of his heart to all generations. Blessed is the nation whose God is the LORD; and the people whom he hath chosen for his own inheritance. The LORD looketh from heaven; he beholdeth all the sons of men. From the place of his habitation he looketh upon all the inhabitants of the earth. He fashioneth their hearts alike; he considereth all their works. . . . Behold, the eye of the LORD is upon them that fear him, upon them that hope in his mercy; To deliver their soul from death, and to keep them alive in famine. Our soul waiteth for the LORD: he is our help and our shield. For our heart shall rejoice in him, because we have trusted in his holy name. Let thy mercy, O LORD, be upon us, according as we hope in thee. (VERSES 1–15, 18–22)

Wizard Island from Discovery Point in Crater Lake National Park, Oregon.
Photograph by Terry Donnelly/Donnelly-Austin Photography

PSALM 47

O CLAP YOUR HANDS, ALL YE PEOPLE; shout unto God with the voice of triumph. For the LORD most high is terrible; he is a great King over all the earth. He shall subdue the people under us, and the nations under our feet. He shall choose our inheritance for us, the excellency of Jacob whom he loved. Selah.

O clap your hands, all ye people; shout unto God with the voice of triumph.

God is gone up with a shout, the LORD with the sound of a trumpet. Sing praises to God, sing praises: sing praises unto our King, sing praises. For God is the King of all the earth: sing ye praises with understanding. God reigneth over the heathen: God sitteth upon the throne of his holiness. The princes of the people are gathered together, even the people of the God of Abraham: for the shields of the earth belong unto God: he is greatly exalted.

Rainbow in Denali National Park, Alaska. Photograph by Carr Clifton

Oh, Worship the King
(PSALM 104)

Robert Grant

Oh, worship the King all glorious above!
Oh, gratefully sing his power and his love—
Our Shield and Defender, the Ancient of Days,
Pavilioned in splendor and girded with praise.

Oh, tell of his might, Oh, sing of his grace,
Whose robe is the light, whose canopy space;
His chariots of wrath the deep thunder-clouds form,
And dark is his path on the wings of the storm.

The earth with its store of wonders untold,
Almighty, thy power hath founded of old,
Hath stablished it fast by a changeless decree,
And round it hath cast, like a mantle, the sea.

Thy bountiful care, what tongue can recite?
It breathes in the air; it shines in the light;
It streams from the hills; it descends to the plain
And sweetly distills in the dew and the rain.

Frail children of dust, and feeble as frail,
In thee do we trust, nor find thee to fail;
Thy mercies how tender, how firm to the end,
Our Maker, Defender, Redeemer, and Friend.

O measureless Might! Ineffable Love!
While angels delight to hymn thee above,
The humbler creation, though feeble their lays,
With true adoration shall sing to thy praise.

Thou Art, O God

Thomas Moore

Thou art, O God, the life and light
Of all this wondrous world we see;
Its glow by day, its smile by night,
Are but reflections caught from thee.
Where'er we turn thy glories shine,
And all things fair and bright are thine!

When day, with farewell beam, delays
Among the opening clouds of even,
And we can almost think we gaze
Through golden vistas into heaven
Those hues that make the sun's decline
So soft, so radiant, Lord, are thine.

When night, with wings of starry gloom,
O'ershadows all the earth and skies,
Like some dark, beauteous bird,
    whose plume
Is sparkling with unnumbered eyes—
That sacred gloom, those fires divine,
So grand, so countless, Lord, are thine.

When youthful Spring around
    us breathes,
Thy spirit warms her fragrant sigh;
And every flower the summer wreathes
Is born beneath that kindling eye.
Where'er we turn, thy glories shine,
And all things fair and bright are thine!

Make a joyful noise unto God, all ye lands.

—PSALM 66:1

Praise to the Creator

Isaac Watts

Ye nations of the earth rejoice
Before the Lord, your sovereign King.
Serve him with cheerful heart and voice;
With all your tongues his glory sing.

The Lord is God; 'tis he alone
Doth life and breath and being give.
We are his work and not our own,
The sheep that on his pasture live.

Enter his gates with songs of joy;
With praises to his courts repair;
And make it your divine employ
To pay your thanks and honours there.

The Lord is good; the Lord is kind.
Great is his grace, his mercy sure;
And the whole race of man shall find
His truth from age to age endure.

We Give Thee Thanks

Thomas Merton

We give thee thanks, O God,
For great moments of joy and strength
That come to us when by a strong
And special movement of grace
We are able to perform some act of pure
And disinterested love.

For the clean fire of that love
Which floods the soul and cleanses
The whole man and leaves us filled with
An unexpected lightness and freedom
        for action.

For the moment of pure prayer
Which not only establishes order in the soul
But even fortifies us against physical weariness
And brings us a new lease on life itself.
Glory be to thee
For thy precious gift!

PSALM 95

O COME, LET US SING UNTO THE LORD: let us make a joyful noise to the rock of our salvation. Let us come before his presence with thanksgiving, and make a joyful noise unto him with psalms. For the LORD is a great God, and a

> O come, let us sing unto the LORD: let us make a joyful noise to the rock of our salvation.

great King above all gods. In his hand are the deep places of the earth: the strength of the hills is his also. The sea is his, and he made it: and his hands formed the dry land.

O come, let us worship and bow down: let us kneel before the LORD our maker. For he is our God; and we are the people of his pasture, and the sheep of his hand. (VERSES 1–7)

Birch trees and sandstone cliffs along Lake Superior, Pictured Rocks National Lakeshore, Michigan. Photograph by Carr Clifton

PSALM *138*

I WILL PRAISE THEE with my whole heart: before the gods will I sing praise unto thee. I will worship toward thy holy temple, and praise thy name for thy lovingkindness and for thy truth: for thou hast magnified thy word above all thy name.

In the day when I cried thou answeredst me, and strengthenedst me with strength in my soul.

All the kings of the earth shall praise thee, O LORD . . .

All the kings of the earth shall praise thee, O LORD, when they hear the words of thy mouth. Yea, they shall sing in the ways of the LORD: for great is the glory of the LORD.

Though the LORD be high, yet hath he respect unto the lowly: but the proud he knoweth afar off.

Though I walk in the midst of trouble, thou wilt revive me: thou shalt stretch forth thine hand against the wrath of mine enemies, and thy right hand shall save me.

The LORD will perfect that which concerneth me: thy mercy, O LORD, endureth for ever: forsake not the works of thine own hands.

Buzzards' Roost, Fall Creek Falls State Park, Tennessee.
Photograph by Carr Clifton

PSALM 148

PRAISE YE THE LORD. Praise ye the LORD from the heavens: praise him in the heights. Praise ye him, all his angels: praise ye him, all his hosts.

Praise ye him, sun and moon: praise him, all ye stars of light. Praise him, ye heavens of heavens, and ye waters that be above the heavens.

> Let them praise the name of the LORD: for his name alone is excellent; his glory is above the earth and heaven.

Let them praise the name of the LORD: for he commanded, and they were created. He hath also stablished them for ever and ever: he hath made a decree which shall not pass.

Praise the LORD from the earth, ye dragons, and all deeps: Fire, and hail; snow, and vapours; stormy wind fulfilling his word: Mountains, and all hills; fruitful trees, and all cedars: Beasts, and all cattle; creeping things, and flying fowl: Kings of the earth, and all people; princes, and all judges of the earth: Both young men, and maidens; old men, and children: Let them praise the name of the LORD: for his name alone is excellent; his glory is above the earth and heaven.

He also exalteth the horn of his people, the praise of all his saints; even of the children of Israel, a people near unto him. Praise ye the LORD.

Redwood trees in California. Photograph © Corbis

O praise the LORD, all ye nations: praise him, all ye people.
For his merciful kindness is great toward us: and the
truth of the LORD endureth for ever. Praise ye the LORD.

—PSALM 117

The Incarnation

Charles Wesley

Glory be to God on high,
And peace on earth descend;
God comes down: he bows the sky
And shows himself our friend!
God the invisible appears,
God the blest, the Great I AM,
Sojourns in this vale of tears,
And Jesus is the name.

Him the angels all adored
Their Maker and their King;
Tidings of their humbled Lord
They now to mortals bring:
Emptied of his majesty,
Of his dazzling glories shorn,
Being's Source begins to be,
And God Himself is born!

See the eternal Son of God,
A mortal son of man,
Dwelling in an earthly clod
Whom heaven cannot contain!
Stand amazed, ye heavens at this!
See the Lord of earth and skies,
Humbled to the dust He is
And in a manger lies!

We the sons of men rejoice,
The Prince of Peace proclaim,
With heaven's host lift up our voice
And shout Immanuel's name;
Knees and hearts to him we bow;
Of our flesh and of our bone,
Jesus is our brother now,
And God is all our own!

Adam's Morning Prayer

John Milton

These are thy glorious works, parent of good,
Almighty! Thine this universal frame,
Thus wondrous fair; thyself how wondrous then!
Unspeakable, who sit'st above these heavens
To us invisible, or dimly seen
In these thy lowest works; yet these declare
Thy goodness beyond thought, and power divine.

Speak, ye who best can tell, ye sons of light,
Angels; for ye behold him, and with songs
And choral symphonies, day without night,
Circle his throne rejoicing, ye in heaven.
On Earth join all ye creatures
To extol him first, him last,
Him midst, and without end.

We Love You, O God

Saint Anselm

We love you, O God;
And we desire to love you more and more.
Grant us that we may love you
As much as we desire, and as much as we ought.

O dearest Friend, who has so loved and saved us,
The thought of whom is so sweet
And always growing sweeter,
Come with Christ and dwell in our hearts;
Then you will keep a watch over our lips,
Our steps, our deeds, and we shall not need to be
Anxious either for our souls or our bodies.

Give us love, sweetest of all gifts,
Which knows no enemy.

Give us in our hearts pure love,
Born of your love to us, that we may
Love others as you love us.

O most loving Father of Jesus Christ,
From whom flows all love,
Let our hearts, frozen in sin,
Cold to you and cold to others,
Be warmed by this divine fire.
So help and bless us in your son. Amen.

PSALM *67*

GOD BE MERCIFUL UNTO US, and bless us; and cause his face to shine upon us; Selah. That thy way may be known upon earth, thy saving health among all nations.

Let the people praise thee, O God; let all the people praise thee. O let the nations be glad and sing for joy: for thou shalt judge the people righteously, and govern the nations upon earth. Selah.

> ## O let the nations be glad and sing for joy . . .

Let the people praise thee, O God; let all the people praise thee. Then shall the earth yield her increase; and God, even our own God, shall bless us. God shall bless us; and all the ends of the earth shall fear him.

Iceberg at sunrise in the Stikine-LeConte Wilderness, Tongass National Forest, Alaska. Photograph by Carr Clifton

PSALM *150*

PRAISE YE THE LORD. Praise God in his sanctuary: praise him in the firmament of his power. Praise him for his mighty acts: praise him according to his excellent greatness.

    Praise him with the sound of the trumpet: praise him with the psaltery and harp. Praise him with the timbrel and dance: praise him

---

Praise him for his mighty acts: praise him according to his excellent greatness.

---

with stringed instruments and organs. Praise him upon the loud cymbals: praise him upon the high sounding cymbals.

    Let every thing that hath breath praise the LORD. Praise ye the Lord.

Heart Lake in Adirondack Park and Preserve,
New York. Photograph by Carr Clifton

PSALM *100*

MAKE A JOYFUL NOISE UNTO the LORD, all ye lands. Serve the LORD with gladness: come before his presence with singing. Know ye that the LORD he is God: it is he that hath made us, and not we ourselves; we are his people, and the sheep of his pasture.

For the LORD is good;
his mercy is everlasting;
and his truth endureth
to all generations.

Enter into his gates with thanksgiving, and into his courts with praise: be thankful unto him, and bless his name.

For the LORD is good; his mercy is everlasting; and his truth endureth to all generations.

Rock formations at Big Sur, California.
Photograph © George Oze Photography/SuperStock

INDEX *of* TITLES, POETS, *and* COMPOSERS

INDEX *of* PSALMS

(Psalm: page number)